Who Is Watching Your Money?

Your Small Business Guide to Profit and Cash Flow

Who Is Watching Your Money?

Your Small Business Guide to Profit and Cash Flow

Belynda de Beurs, CPA, CGA

YouSpeakIt
PUBLISHING
*The Easy Way
to Get Your Book
Done Right!*™

www.YouSpeakItPublishing.com

Copyright © 2017 Belynda de Beurs

All rights reserved. No part of this book may be reproduced or transmitted in any form or by any means without written permission of the publisher, except in the case of brief quotations embodied in critical articles and reviews.

This material has been written and published solely for educational purposes. The author and the publisher shall have neither liability nor responsibility to any person or entity with respect to any loss, damage, or injury caused or alleged to be caused directly or indirectly by the information contained in this book.

Statements made and opinions expressed in this publication are those of the author and do not necessarily reflect the views of the publisher or indicate an endorsement by the publisher.

ISBN: 978-1-945446-30-6

I'd like to dedicate this book to my husband Richard, for his unwavering love and support. Without him, my journey thus far would not have been possible. Thank you.

To my daughter, Michaela, who hates accounting, but grasped the concepts of cash management and cost control at an early age. Way to go.

To my son Alexander, who always stays true to himself and has a heart of gold. You rock.

Acknowledgments

I'd like to acknowledge:

My parents, for instilling strong core values in me right from the beginning.

My Certified General Accounting (CGA) professor, for throwing those chocolate bars across the exam room so I could push through the grueling three-hour national exams.

My first boss after I graduated, who taught me how to be a leader and a mentor to others.

My business coach, who showed me that an accounting designation opens up a whole world of opportunities, and not only in accounting.

Lastly, my branding coach, who grounded me and helped me find my true passion in a style that was all my own.

Contents

Introduction

You are facing a challenge in your company. Chances are that your problems involve either cash flow or profitability; otherwise, you would not be reading this book.

Are you a small business owner who has dreams of financial freedom?

Have you become frustrated with a lack of results?

Are you finally ready to take it up a notch and get serious about achieving your goals?

This book was written to help you. It has been designed to address the most common struggles that business owners have with cash flow and profit. Included within these chapters are tools and resources that will help you to make strategic improvements to your business so that you can overcome cash and profit challenges.

Moreover, this book provides a holistic framework to support long-lasting solutions. Besides helping you to solve your business problems, I will teach you how to prevent those challenges from ever returning.

Increasing your bottom line is a huge priority for you, as a business owner — or it should be. Included within this book are suggestions on how to make this happen both efficiently and effectively.

This book will help you explore the six key components of the profit formula and to evaluate the six key foundations of your business that will become the heartbeat of your success.

I'd like to take a few moments to look at the dynamics of your small business. Based on my experience in working with business owners, the fact that you picked up this book means that the following facts are likely to be true.

See if any of this sounds familiar:

- Your business is relatively new—less than ten years old—and you have fewer than ten employees.

- When you started the business, you had a dream. You wanted to work for yourself because, frankly, working for someone else and seeing them rake in all the dough was not appealing to you anymore.

- You were full of excitement at your business launch, and the opportunities seemed endless, but then things started to change.

- You noticed that you were starting to work longer hours than you did as an employee.

- You had business start-up costs that seemed to come out of nowhere.

- You hired a couple of staff members to help with the workload, which made perfect sense at the time, but still, you found yourself putting in many extra hours of overtime.

- After all this effort, your take-home pay was not much more than what you were making as an employee.

How much of this applies to you?

These are common circumstances.

What happens in small businesses to create this situation?

Well, business life happens. There are sales to think about, customers to keep happy, grievances, and other staffing issues to handle, financial numbers to interpret, banking relationships to maintain, and the taxman to deal with. As any business progresses, financial calculations become more complex, and planning becomes more difficult. On top of everything else, business owners are under constant pressure, especially if there are cash flow problems.

You wonder: *Where are the profits I thought would be coming in?*

You could be thinking: *Maybe it would be easier going back to being just an employee.*

If you are thinking this way, then maybe you need to stop and take a breather. Don't give up. You have a great company, and there are customers who need what you sell. You are employing people and making an impact in their lives. You are making a difference in the world around you.

Instead of raising the white flag, you need to change your focus. Refocus on the things that matter most to your business, those things that will pay you dividends at the end of the day.

After twenty-five years of working as a financial accountant and consultant, I have developed a three-dimensional profit formula that will drive significant results straight to your bottom line. It will change the way you think about your business. It's your turn to reap the rewards, and we can do it together, by focusing on what keeps the wheels turning — your cash and your profit.

To achieve the results that you are looking for, however, you must be prepared to put in the necessary time and effort. Applying the methods and recommendations in this book will take determination, energy, and a commitment to the process. There are questions at the end of each chapter that have been included to point your thinking in the right direction. In order to get the most out of the book, I highly recommend that you put serious thought into completing these exercises.

I wrote this book because I am truly passionate about this content. I have developed an approach that can turn businesses from red to black, and I am thrilled to share it with you. The content has been carefully selected to show you where you can act to improve your cash flow and make more money for your business. It is practical advice, based on my twenty-five years of business and accounting experience.

The methods in this book are general, so they can be applied to different kinds of businesses. However, each business field has its own requirements and constraints, and each individual company has unique circumstances.

This book does not replace the need to seek professional advice from someone who can counsel you about the specifics of your business, review your numbers, and apply strategies to your unique business situation. I encourage you to learn and use the strategies in this book, and to use common sense when applying the methods to your business. Seek independent professional advice if circumstances so warrant.

With that in mind, be prepared to step out of your comfort zone and into your creative zone as we explore some eye-opening topics together. By the time you reach the end of the book, you will be ready to move forward; you will be able to use the contents within the book as your roadmap to profit.

The challenges that you are experiencing are common to most businesses. When you become aware of why you have them and what to do about them, you will then be empowered to become successful. This involves the development of what I call a *gap map.*

It is a three-part process:

1. You must develop an awareness of your current state.

2. You must have a clear end goal in mind.

3. You must be able to connect the first two ideas with purpose-driven action.

As you read this book and work on the exercises, you will collect the necessary information required to run your business effectively. You will start to understand the story behind your business, and this will empower you to be proactive rather than reactive. You will establish your baseline vision of the future and uncover any roadblocks that may be in your way. Then, with a new clarity of vision, you can focus on the opportunities in front of you.

After reading this book and taking part in the activities within, it is my hope that you will use what you have learned to break through your barriers and become a champion of your own success.

- Are you ready for huge paydays and lots of thought-provoking ideas?

- Are you ready to take the next step that your business is craving?

- Are you ready to improve the financial health of your business and increase your profits exponentially?

- Are you ready to commit to working on your business, not just in it?

If so, this is the right book for you. Let's begin.

CHAPTER ONE

Where Is the Focus on Your Money?

WHO'S WATCHING IT?

Who is watching your money?

Can you answer this question with certainty?

Most small business owners cannot. This is a surprisingly common problem, and it can get a company into hot water in a very short time. Cash is the lifeblood of your business—it is the very thing that keeps your business running—and yet, it is unlikely to be managed conscientiously. In my experience with small businesses, I have found that the chain of responsibility for cash management is often unclear.

Think about what you know about cash management in your business. As the business owner, you probably know bits and pieces, here and there, but consider this question carefully:

Who has the full responsibility of managing cash for your business?

It is important to understand who is watching your money for the very reason it is important to have the right amount of blood pumping through your bloodstream. All transactions within your organization run on cash—either current or future balances—and in order for you to run your business effectively, you need to have the right amount at the right time in the right place.

Who's really watching your money?

Let's try to answer this question.

It's Not Your Year-End Accountant

You probably have an accountant whom you see about your year-end financial situation.

What does this accountant do, and how do they impact your business?

What kind of interaction do you have with your year-end accountant?

There is a reason they are called a year-end accountant, and that is because you see them once a year. Picture yourself at the dreaded year-end meeting with your accountant. It's likely that you don't really understand what the accountant is talking about. You probably can't interpret the financial statements yourself. You may not even care to try.

During your meeting, the accountant may speak to you for quite a while, but you are probably only listening for a few key pieces of information:

- Did you make money this year?
- How much in taxes do you owe?
- How much is the accountant going to cost you this time?

You probably look at the whole process as a necessary evil, and breathe a sigh of relief as you leave the office with your year-end documents in your briefcase. Chances are, as soon as you walk out of your accountant's office, you will have forgotten most of what was talked about.

What do you do with the financial information you have been given when you get back to your office?

The documents probably get filed away in a binder on a shelf, collecting dust until the next year-end rolls around, and you go through the process all over again.

Is there valuable information in those documents?

Of course. You've selected an expert in the field to be your year-end accountant and the documents you've been handed can give you important information about your business.

Why, then, do these pages stay on the shelf?

For many small business owners, there is a disconnect between the *numbers* on the pages and the *story* the numbers are telling. The year-end accountant provides you with your year-end numbers. If you are the owner of a business, it is your responsibility to understand the story that these numbers tell—especially the ones that are vital to the operation of your business.

Back to our original question—is this accountant watching your cash?

Well, although this person has expertise in the field, you know you only see your year-end accountant once a year. You also know that adequate cash levels are required throughout the entire year for you to run your business, so your year-end accountant most definitely is not the person who is watching your cash.

It's Not Your Bookkeeper

If you are a small business owner, and you have been in business for five years or so, chances are you have a small, internal accounting department. It is probably made up of one or two people.

These are the common characteristics of this department:

- The responsibilities of the staff are largely administrative.

24

- Staff members push paper every day from one side of the desk to the other, making sure invoices are paid and money is collected.

- The business credit card statements and bank statements are probably balanced monthly.

- If you are lucky, the staff ensures that all your government remittances are accurate and paid on time.

- Using accounting software, income reports are probably generated, hopefully with some regularity.

Accounting software enables a person to push a button and get a set of financial statements, which will include a balance sheet and an income statement. Your bookkeeper does not have to know what is included in these statements; the process is automated for them.

You may think that your bookkeeper is watching your cash, but rarely, if ever, will accounting software produce a cash flow statement. Your bookkeeper, therefore, would have to generate this kind of statement from scratch. To create it, they would have to know how to select appropriate data and insert it into a software platform—an Excel spreadsheet, for example—and manipulate the data properly to get meaningful results.

The bookkeeper would need to understand both the data and the use of the program in order to create an accurate cash flow statement.

At this point, you may be asking yourself: *Is my bookkeeper qualified enough?*

It is a good question to ask.

Here are some items for you to consider:

- When your bookkeeper produces financial statements, do you receive them in a timely manner?

- Does the bookkeeper understand the content?

- Can you understand the content?

- Is your bookkeeper able to explain all the components of the financials to you?

If you can't answer *yes* to these questions with confidence, it isn't surprising.

You must keep in mind that even the smartest bookkeeper is still only a technician in the organizational structure of your company. They do not have knowledge of the details of the other branches of your business. They do not have access to your history, your research, your short- or long-term business plans, your production needs, or your future projections for money, supplies, and staff.

So, should you be relying on your bookkeeper for your cash flow information?

Let's use a medical analogy: If you had a medical condition, would you rely on a lab technician to diagnose you and explain your treatment options?

Or would you rather have a doctor — a specialist in the field — give you the information?

In a small business, a bookkeeper — who is not a designated accountant — can't adequately explain the financial health of your company to you, and they can't possibly help you understand what your cash position will be in three months or a year from now. This level of understanding is vital to your business.

One more note: new business owners often don't invest enough in their accounting resources simply because they are not income generating. I am here to tell you that there is an untapped potential in this area, just waiting to be discovered.

Most small business owners undervalue the importance of accurate cash flow information, but it is a key to managing your business effectively. We will come back to this later in the book.

For now, we've just uncovered that your bookkeeper is most likely not managing your cash either. Yikes!

Chances Are, It's Not You

Let's do a little bit of self-reflection about your current responsibilities. If you own your own business, you wear many hats. Your focus will vary, depending on the day, month, or season. One day, you may be focused on sales. The next day, you may be focused on operations, or your product line, or you may be dealing with customer issues. You are pulled in all different directions, day by day, depending on what comes across your desk.

Are you watching the money?

You know that you need cash to operate your business, and you hope at the end of the month that there is enough to pay everyone, but you are not really watching it every day. It is understandably difficult for business owners to manage cash flow themselves.

Here are some of the reasons why you might find it challenging:

- Numbers are not your forte.
- You don't know what you should be watching.
- It is a difficult task to keep track of cash flow.
- You don't have the time to do this job.

- You don't fully understand the difference between cash flow and profit.

Understanding numbers is probably not your forte. This is true of most entrepreneurs. To complete all the compilations necessary to determine cash flow, you need a full understanding of the numbers. If you are honest with yourself, you will acknowledge that this is not your strength.

Regarding cash management, it may not be difficult to assess when you need more cash, but you also need to be able to tell when you have excess sitting around doing nothing, and when it is time to use that excess to move your business forward.

The ins and outs of cash flow can be hard to follow consistently, but it must be done. Too often, business people don't place enough importance on this task, choosing to focus instead on the amount of money they have at any one time. It may surprise you to know that it is not the amount of money in your bank that is important; it is the *transactions* taking place that are key to the health of the business.

A common problem I see is that business owners think that if they have money in their bank account, their company has profit. However, cash is *not* profit, and we will get to that discussion later in the book.

To sum up this section, we have seen that your year-end accountant is not watching your money, nor is your bookkeeper. You don't have the time, nor is it your general nature to watch cash. You know that it's important that somebody be watching your money.

So, who is watching it?

Let's continue by asking: *Who needs to know the status of your cash flow?*

WHO NEEDS TO KNOW ABOUT IT?

You know that watching your company's money — and understanding what's happening — is necessary for a lot of reasons.

Now, change your perspective for a moment, and think about this from another side:

Who needs to know your cash position?

Because we know that no one is really watching the money levels in your business right now — not at the level that it deserves — it can be helpful to understand who actually needs to know your cash status.

Who is likely to be interested in where your cash is sitting?

Who would want to know when you have excess cash and who wants to know when you are short?

Who is affected by changes in your cash flow?

All businesses function on cash. People inside your business need to know about it; people outside your business need to know about it. It is the lifeblood of your business, and its fluctuations affect other people and other businesses.

Cash goes in and out of your business constantly and it is always a two-sided transaction. Someone on the other side of your transaction is affected one way or another. If they are going to be affected by it — whether positively or negatively — you'd better believe that they are going to want to keep track of your cash position.

Your Bank and Lenders Need to Know

First and foremost, your bank and your lenders need to know your cash status at any given time. All business owners will be short of cash at times and will need to borrow.

For example:

- You may have start-up costs that exceed your capital.

- You may be caught off guard with an unexpected expense.

- You may you need to make a large purchase and require a bit more cash than what you have in the bank at that time.

Once you enter into a contract or agreement with a lender, you can bet they will be requiring certain timely reports to ensure you are using the funds for the intended purpose.

For example, if you get an operating loan, you need to make sure that it's for the operations of your business. You would not be able to spend it, for instance, on a capital purchase like buying a company truck. You will need to keep records of your expenditures. If they have given you an operating line, the bank is going to want to see your financial statements on a regular basis to make sure the money is being used in an appropriate manner.

I have seen many misappropriations of borrowed cash in the past and it never pays off. If you spent your operation funds on a truck, as in the example we gave above, eventually you will actually need money for operations, say to buy inventory. If you are short of cash once again, the bank will often not make a second loan.

The bank will also be watching your cash because they want to make sure you can afford your monthly interest payments. This means that the company must be generating enough new cash through the day-to-day operations to cover the interest payments for the loan they have given you.

Your Business Needs to Know

There is a common saying: *Cash is king.*

All businesses run on cash.

Without it, your business won't last long, and your doors will close. Cash comes in and cash goes out. It's an endless cycle.

For the health of your business, the question you need to be able to answer is:

What is the right cash amount to keep your business running at an optimal level?

Depending on the type of business you have, your cash position could fluctuate a bit from one month to another. Let's assume your business is running on a steady amount of cash. You think things are going smoothly, and suddenly, an unexpected expense hits you. Growing your business responsibly means having access to cash when and where you need it. If you are financially prepared for the unexpected, you have a better chance of negotiating a more favorable interest rate with your bank.

Robbing Peter to Pay Paul: An Example of Improper Cash Flow Management

A company I once worked for had multiple projects running at the same time. Each project had its own separate cash flow. They didn't understand the importance of keeping these cash flows separate from each other, so all the cash went into one general account.

This created a bad cash-flow situation; they were robbing Peter to pay Paul in their business operations. That is a definite no-no. Make sure you understand your business, how it operates, and the cash management that is required in your business as a whole, and for any individual projects that you may have.

Obviously, *You* Need to Know

Most small businesses require business loans. When a business owner acquires a business loan, it's usually secured by some form of personal guarantee.

In small businesses, personal finances are strongly connected to the business finances. As a business owner, then, when you personally guarantee a loan, your personal assets will be at risk if your business doesn't perform.

If your business is short of cash, guess whom the bank will ask to make up that shortfall?

That's right. You. It is vital that you be aware of the cash flow in your company because it may directly affect your personal finances.

In addition, your company provides you with income, and the system you use for payment is important. Small business owners often don't manage their own salaries properly, and this can result in significant cash flow problems.

How do you get paid by your company?

If you are incorporated, you will draw either a salary or dividends, or you may tap in to your previous shareholder loan. Usually, business owners end up setting up a system in which they get paid last — if there is any money left. In some companies I have worked for in the past, the owner has gone almost a whole year without paying himself. You want your business to succeed, but, like everyone else, you have your own personal expenses at home to pay, so not paying yourself is impractical.

It's crucial to understand how much cash you actually have in the company at any given time. Leaving your salary out of the equation makes this impossible. It's unrealistic to expect that you are not going to draw some form of compensation. You need to put this compensation into company financial projections.

Paying Yourself: Example of Improper Owner Compensation

I want to tell you a story about another company I worked with. The owners of the company were not paying attention to the cash flow. Although the operations of the business were not generating enough cash for the owners to withdraw money, the owners withdrew the money anyway, in order to pay their mortgages and other expenses. Then, they couldn't figure out why there wasn't enough money in the bank account to pay their subcontractors and suppliers.

As a small business owner, you must not mix your personal and business cash. Manage your salary so that you can protect yourself and be sure you have sufficient funds to take care of your own expenses. This will require some careful planning.

PAST, PRESENT, AND FUTURE

To know as much as possible about your cash flow in any business, financial reports are essential, and they must be designed to help you answer three questions:

- Where has your cash been?
- Where is your cash now?
- Where is your cash going in the future?

As an entrepreneur, you need to have access to specific financial reports, and the timing of reporting is critical to your understanding of the health and direction of your business. Think of the reports like the information you find on the dashboard of your car. Some information must be kept at your fingertips if you are to manage your company efficiently and profitably.

What are your dashboard reports?

Think about this question as we proceed. You will find suggestions about reports to keep on your dashboard as you read ahead.

You can extract different kinds of information from different kinds of reports.

The three kinds of reporting that give you time-based information are:

- Historical reporting
- Current reporting
- Future forecasting

Historical Reporting

Earlier in this chapter, we briefly spoke about the differing roles of the year-end accountant and the bookkeeper. They are similar in that both provide information about your business, and that information is historical. They provide details about what has happened in the past, whether it was last week, last month, or last year. This is referred to as historical reporting.

Historical reporting, even though it is limited to what happened in the past, is valuable for many reasons:

- The data in historical reports allows you to do variance reporting, trend analyses, and year-over-year comparisons.

- Historical reports can tell you what you are doing right — and where you are truly excelling.

- They can tell you what you have done wrong, and which strategies or products have not been successful.

- Historical reporting will allow accountants to do what we call *vertical and horizontal analyses*.

- Historical reports can compare what your expenses are as a percentage of sales on a profit and loss statement.

- With historical data, you can do a balance sheet comparison of what your debt is to your equity or what your current assets are to your current liabilities.

There is a lot of value in historical reporting, and it is where most business owners focus their attention.

However, it's like driving a car without headlights. You don't know where you are going, and you don't know where you are. You only know where you've been. Your knowledge is only as good as the last road sign you saw before the lights went out.

The past is the past; it's over. It's good to know about, but you can't do anything about it. Where you're headed is what really matters.

This Year's Numbers

Let's assume that you are taking a proactive approach with your financial numbers. You have a solid understanding of how much money you've been making on a month-to-month basis. If you take your monthly numbers and multiply by twelve, you can calculate a projected number for the year. You can work with your sales team to estimate what your sales are going to be.

Using a past *trend analysis* will allow you to be informed enough to project some costs associated with delivering your product. You estimate your monthly overhead — costs related to items like rent, staffing, marketing, and travel — to be a certain average amount per month. Again, you take that number, and multiply it by twelve to estimate your costs for a year.

Seems like you can pretty easily project out what you think your next twelve months will end up looking like, right?

Nope, wrong.

Here are just a few examples of what you may have forgotten:

- You are offering an additional product this coming year.

- You are moving offices halfway through the year.

- You have additions to your team.

- Your newly bought truck needs additional insurance coverage.

- Your suppliers have announced a price increase.

- Your operations team now has a new staff member, so production times have just increased by 10 percent.

- And, oh yeah—the taxman just increased corporate tax by 1 percent.

Your simple, wing-it approach to understanding how much cash you will have in twelve months, and how much profit you have left to pay yourself, has just rewarded you with a big gray area.

I can't stress enough how crucial it is that you ensure your financial numbers are as accurate as possible. Make the investment. Give this area your focus and attention, and you will have the best chance of making good decisions when it comes to running your business.

You do need to pay attention to the present cash flow numbers, but I hope it is apparent to you that they only tell you a small part of the story of your business finances.

When you are focused on this year's numbers, it's like you are driving in your car and your headlights are on, but it's dark outside. You can see as far as your headlights will allow you, but if there are any turns up ahead, you can't see around them at all.

So, what do you need if you are driving this way?

You need a roadmap, so to speak—or a GPS—that will help you see the road ahead. You need some information that will help you get around the corner and safely to your destination.

Future Forecasting

Future forecasting is all about looking into the future.

Where are you headed?

What does the future look like?

Future forecasting requires that you identify your destination or goals, and plan how to get there. You need experience and expertise to be able to anticipate bumps and turns along the way. This is known as strategic thinking.

Strategic Thinking: Examples of Companies Looking into the Future

One company I worked for was looking to grow, so they needed to look into the future as far as they could. There are different ways to grow a business, and they had chosen to look into the option of purchasing another company in order to expand into a different region. Many matters needed to be considered and money was obviously an important one. Cash would be required, and financing would be necessary. To make this purchase decision, a large cash flow projection needed to be made for three years in advance to make sure that it was a viable proposal.

Because they invested in this kind of research, this company was able to establish that this was a good investment, and, as a result, their revenue grew to five times its original value in less than three years.

Another company I worked with had been in business for twenty-five years. We hit a significant recession in the Calgary market, due to declining oil prices.

What do you do when an external force hits your company like this?

When the norm is no longer valid, you need to be able to make adjustments, and you may have to react quickly. You can't do this unless you know where you're going.

Do you have a plan?

Do you have a clear destination?

Have you laid out your short- and long-term goals?

If you can answer *yes* to these questions, you are much more likely to be able to adapt to a changing landscape like this company did. They were able to stay viable through the recession when other businesses failed.

Part of future forecasting is keeping your eyes and ears open from an accounting point of view. It's about constant communication within your team, your department, and your business as a whole, as well as with external partners, such as your bank and other support institutions.

Historical reporting, current reporting, and future forecasting are all required for a holistic approach to money management. Together, they will help you keep your focus on the critical areas of your business.

Historical reporting will help you understand trend analyses. These reports will tell you where you have been so you can see which strategies have been successful and which have not. *Current reporting* will enable you to make timely adjustments so you can be as successful as you can in the current year. *Future forecasting* will ensure that you reach your business goals and objectives in the future.

Before you move on to the next chapter, make a conscious investment in strengthening your business. Take the time to thoroughly think about and answer the questions in the exercises at the end of each chapter. The more thought you put into it, the more you will get out of it. The answers will help you develop your action plan by the end of the book.

CHAPTER ONE EXERCISES

- Whom are you going to empower to watch and monitor your money from today on?

- What additional training does your bookkeeper require?

- What information do you need from your accountant that you are not currently getting?

- Are you setting aside time to monitor your cash situation?

- Do you know what information your bank/lenders need and when they are going to need it?

- Are you combining project cash flows for different projects, or are you keeping them separate?

- How much money do you require, personally, out of the business, and when do you need it?

- What percentage of your financial reports is historical reporting, and what percentage is guiding you to your future?

CHAPTER TWO

Where Is the Money, and Where Is It Going?

SOURCES AND USES OF CASH

Earlier on, I mentioned that all businesses need cash to operate. Cash flows in and out of the company on a regular basis. If you understand the activities of your business that provide and require cash, you can prepare ahead of time for your cash needs, and you won't ever be caught off guard.

The common report that most accountants provide at the end of the year is called a *statement of cash position.*

Do you receive this report?

If you didn't ask for it, you might not be getting it. Even when it is provided, most business owners overlook the valuable information in their statement of cash position.

Let's talk about what this report contains.

There are three basic components:

- Operating activities
- Financing activities
- Investing activities

I will go into detail regarding each section. Although you may receive this statement at the end of the year, I want you to understand how the information in this report impacts you today — at this very moment.

Operating Activities

Operating activities represent those activities that are carried out in your day-to-day business.

Examples include:

- Your sales transactions
- Your expenses
- Your overhead costs

Your sales transactions are tracked through invoices, your expenses are your production costs, and your overhead costs describe payments that keep your business doors open. You can see that these are all cash flow activities.

Simply put, when you put them together, these items represent your net income for running your business. If you have a positive net income, where revenue exceeds cost, then your cash balance will go up, and vice versa.

When you are looking at your cash position, be sure you are considering the difference between making and losing money, and fluctuations in your cash balance.

For example, if the business has a debt outstanding and you make a payment on this balance, you haven't really lost any money, but you have had cash leave your business. Similarly, if someone has owed you money for a while, when they pay you, your business hasn't made any money, but your cash balance has gone up.

Do you know what transactions are providing money to your business?

Do you know what transactions are draining money from your business?

Having this knowledge will enable you to manage your cash position in a controlled and disciplined way. Take a moment to reflect on your current operating activities and the impact that they are having on your cash balance as of today.

Financing Activities

Some of the money that flows in and out of any business is due to financing activities. Examples are personal loans, bank financing, and mortgages. A company may borrow money, or it may lend money — to an individual or to another business. If you are a small business owner, chances are good that your significant financing activities represent loans you have had to establish to run your business.

Any time you receive a loan advance or make a loan payment, the transaction involves cash, and this will affect the availability of cash to run the operations of your business.

These are four concepts you should be aware of when reflecting on your financing activities and we will discuss each of these in the paragraphs that follow:

- The terms of your loans
- The security of your loans
- The cost of your loans
- The timing of your loan advances

A lender will establish the terms of your loan, including an expiration date. You will, of course, need to pay your loan back at some point in time. You always need to be aware of when your loan is going to expire so that you can prepare for payment.

Is your loan due on demand?

If it is, the lender could call your loan at *any* time, and you must be prepared to pay.

Most loans require security — you were probably asked to specify some sort of collateral before you took the loan. If you fail to make a payment on time due to insufficient cash on hand, the bank could take your secured item as collateral.

There are many types and structures of loan agreements, but all of them involve some cost. The general rule is that the cost of your loan correlates with how risky it is to the lender. Cash payments are determined not only by the negotiated interest rate, but also by the length of the loan. Most loans require payments to be a blend of both principal and interest.

Be sure you fully understand the timing of your loan advances. Some loans are required for the operations of your business and can be structured as an operating loan. This means you can draw on the loan to pay bills as they come in.

However, the vendors you are buying from won't necessarily have payment terms that are in line with your lender's timing. The bank may not advance you the money early enough to pay the vendor's bill on time. Sometimes, in fact, the bank will require proof of payment to vendors or suppliers *first* before they will transfer money into your account. In these cases, you need to ensure that you can cover one payment period on your own.

You can see how financing activities can affect your cash balance significantly and why you need to be aware of what is happening in relation to those activities today —

not just at the end of the year when your accountant provides your year-end cash report. Take a moment to reflect on your financing activities and the impact they have on your cash flow today.

Investing Activities

We have discussed operating activities and financing activities. The third and last type of activity that can provide or require cash is investments. Depending on the type of business you own, this may be a smaller section of the cash report relative to the number of transactions, but it could have the biggest impact on your business. It requires your full attention.

Many of your efforts for your business can be described as *investments,* but the investing activities in this discussion are those that are not in your main line of work. If your company's main line of work is actually buying and selling investments, then that really has to do with the operations of your business and is covered in the first section of this chapter.

This section refers specifically to investment money coming in and out of your business.

Some common examples are:

- Investments from a third party
- Purchases or sales of shares of your organization

- Investments your company makes in another company, related or unrelated
- Puchases your company makes that are long-term investments, such as buildings, bonds, or other investment funds

Investor money is generally the most expensive method of raising money to finance your business. It is held or borrowed for longer periods of time and can involve larger lump sum payments or transactions flowing in and out of your business. Usually there is substantial paperwork involved, which calls for the assistance of a third-party lawyer. This requires additional money and involves other costs, which can delay the timing of receiving the investment money.

Investor Money and Cash Flow: Avoid Errors in Paperwork and Cash Management

A company that I worked for as chief financial officer (CFO) once had a large project underway. They had done their homework; the project was viable, and research showed it would generate profit for the company. They had met with investors, and had raised the required capital to get the project going. The company had also arranged for an operating loan from the bank for when the project started construction.

The owners of the company were confident that the project would make money. Because they were sure that the money would be coming in, they felt free to buy a significant dollar amount in inventory, using the cash they had on hand from the general operations of their business. This drained their cash in other areas of the business, like paying staff, paying rent, and working on another project.

Unfortunately, it turned out that the investor documentation had not been completed in full, and the commitment was actually never given. The company was in a sticky situation. Fortunately for them, another investor stepped up to the plate, and everything turned out all right.

In this case, the company had a profitable model, but timing and the creation of an unexpected shortage of cash not only jeopardized the project, but also the stability of the company.

Take a moment to reflect on the investments that are currently a part of your business as of today.

What impact are your investments having on your cash balance?

VISUAL CASH VERSUS HIDDEN CASH

It's important to understand the difference between *visual cash* and *hidden cash*. Visual cash is front and center — it is easy to see and is easily accessible. Hidden cash, however, can make you vulnerable to surprises that can catch you off guard.

The Cash Accounts You Know About

Let's talk for a moment about your cash accounts. Every business owner knows about their common cash accounts. You probably get monthly updates on each of them.

The visual accounts that most small businesses have are:

- A general checking account
- A savings account
- One or more operating line accounts

Your general bank account is usually a *checking* account. This is the account that takes all the deposits, and from which the bills get paid. Checks go in and out of this account regularly. Your bookkeeper should be keeping it reconciled on a monthly basis, if not more frequently.

You may have a second bank account that is set aside for *savings*. This account usually has only a few transactions going through it. It probably holds any excess cash you have on a given date. If you do hold a savings account, it's important to make sure that it's working for you. Most savings accounts generate little, if any, interest. Chances are good that your money could be working harder somewhere else in your business. I recommend using this account to help you set aside funds for tax planning initiatives, which we will address later in the book.

Another account that most businesses have is an *operating line*. This account is set up to manage money that is loaned to your business by a creditor, and it fluctuates as money is needed for specific operating expenses.

This account is generally set up to feed automatically into your checking account. If it is working efficiently, you will see daily or weekly automatic transactions flow through this account to your checking account. It is important to keep an eye on this account because every operating line has a maximum limit. You are expected to know what this limit is and how close you are to it at all times.

Companies who are running multiple projects may be required by their banks to maintain separate checking accounts for each project. If you have a good relationship with your bank, you may be able to negotiate your way out of this requirement. Business owners often want to avoid this constraint because of the extra administrative pressure it has on accounting staff — routine monitoring and reporting take a great deal more time when you manage multiple accounts.

On the positive side, however, using multiple accounts can be helpful in several ways:

- You can manage your project cash flow in a more disciplined fashion and keep better track of progress.

- Mixing the cash flow from different projects can be a slippery slope — it may result in your company using cash from one project to finance another, which is not the intended use of the loan funds.

- Mixing cash flow can get businesses into hot water; you can run out of cash quickly if you are not careful.

- When you mix the money, the warning signs that tell you a project is not performing well can easily be masked by another project that is.

The Black Holes: Other Things That Tie Up Your Money

In your business, just like in your personal life, it can sometimes seem like mysterious black holes are absorbing your money, leaving you to wonder where it went.

Where does it go?

Large sums of money—or small sums of money that can add up to significant amounts—can be spent without anyone being fully aware of the extent of the expenditures. Money can also be tied up in investments that were poorly timed, or in purchases that were made without properly assessing cash flow.

To start, let's talk about those automated payments that come out of your account every month or regularly appear on your corporate credit card. As business owners, we all like using the corporate credit card because of the reward points it gives us. However, if you don't keep track, you won't realize what you have spent until the credit card bill comes in.

When the bill does come, business bookkeepers usually reconcile the credit card, and make lump sum payments. At that point, the business owner can completely lose track of the individual costs that racked up the bill to begin with. A lot of companies will pay for things like utilities, mortgage payments, loan interest, lease payments, and even rent with their credit cards. If you don't have a system for tracking or monitoring those expenses against some type of budget, the cost could easily get out of control.

Where else does your money go?

Some one-time transactions can be problematic, if they involved a cash purchase. I am talking about the piece of furniture you bought, or that new computer, or that photocopier sitting around the corner. After a couple months go by, you may forget that they cost you a significant amount of money.

How about the second-hand truck that you bought with cash?

These purchases can be a challenge for a small business when they drain too much cash from the reserve. If the business has used their operating cash to purchase costly items, the cash balance can be unexpectedly depleted, leaving too little to run the operations of their business. There are banks that will lend small businesses cash for exactly these types of purchases. It may be better to use a loan to help you, rather than depleting your cash reserves.

If you have a lot of cash lying around, then—no problem—go ahead and use it for purchases. Using your cash will save you money in interest costs. If, however, you don't plan properly, it may cost you more money in the long run—when you run out of cash and need to borrow at a higher rate to keep your business running.

Some Cash Investments Don't Pay: An Example

After a year of good revenue, a company I know bought a fleet of company vehicles. Although vehicles can be useful, and may be necessary for many company pursuits, they are often not the best investment strategy because they depreciate in value quickly.

What do you think happened the next year when the market turned?

Sales stopped coming in, and soon the company had to downsize. In need of some quick cash, they were forced to sell some of their fleet inventory after only twelve months, and they didn't get very much for them. Sometimes it's better to make business decisions on a cash basis versus a cost basis, and this is a prime example of such a situation.

Contracts That Commit You to Future Spending

In this section, I am going to highlight some key areas of your business in which your future cash has already been committed.

These include:

- Insurance premiums
- Insurance deductibles
- Lease contracts
- Warranty and service contracts
- Employee contracts

All companies require a certain amount of insurance to operate. When you commit to buying an insurance policy, you are committing to not only this month's payment, but also to many payments still to come. The premium payments usually persist as long as you hold the policy, so this is a long-term cash commitment.

In the case of insurance, you are exposed to an additional cost risk, in the form of your deductible — the amount that you would have to pay before the insurance company would pay out on a claim. When I worked in the construction/real estate industry in the past, it was evident that this had a direct impact on the business's cash flow. When a residential unit burned down, for instance, the deductible had to be paid, resulting in tens of thousands of dollars of drainage in cash flow and profit.

Rental lease contracts are another substantial commitment to future cash payments, and this can be especially problematic for small businesses. Your business may grow faster than you anticipate, or have space requirements that weren't predicted. If you have a ten-year lease contract, and your business either outgrows or no longer requires the space, you still must honor your lease commitment.

A Costly Move: Example of the Impact of Long-Term Contracts on Cash Flow

For example, one of the companies I worked for had been leasing office space, but when the business started to take off, the decision was made to purchase a building instead. Once the move was made to the new building, the old lease space went on the market. It wasn't an ideal location, so there was little interest. It was also during a slow economic period, in which it is always difficult to find renters for office space.

There were nine years left on the lease, and this lease was costing ten thousand dollars per month just to stay vacant. It took two and a half years to rent the space out, and even at that, only half of it got rented. This meant a huge cash loss for the company.

Warranty and service contracts also leave the company open to extra cash expenditures. Most businesses that provide a product will offer some sort of warranty or service for that item. If your business provides a warranty, you must factor the future costs into the price of the product.

If you've gotten your budgeting right, this should come out okay in the end. You may win on some items — if they don't need servicing much, or at all — and you will lose on others, but if you've planned right, it will balance out. Of course, it all depends on the quality of your specific product, as well as market timing and other circumstances, some of which are beyond your control.

Warranty Issues Can Cause Cash Losses: Two Examples

Look at the 2016 Samsung phone recall challenge. The cost to the company for replacement phones, the recall process, and massive administrative expenses for following up with those users not wanting to return their devices must have been astronomical. In this case, the extra cash costs to this company resulted from an unforeseen flaw in the product itself.

For another illustration, consider a homebuilder who builds in a high upswing of the market. Under these conditions, it is likely that this business would experience trade shortages, higher production costs, and reduced quality due to the supply and demand factor. Combine that with a couple years of bad environmental weather patterns, and suddenly, the warranty costs can go through the roof — no pun intended — resulting in a large drain in both cash and profit. In this example, market timing and weather circumstances both impacted the cash expenditures in a way the business owner may not have predicted.

Employment contracts can also lead a company exposed to large cash payouts if there is a provision in the contracts for a severance package. When a catastrophic circumstance causes a company to lay off multiple staff members, paying the severance can be very costly.

During a recent oil price plunge in Alberta, for example, a lot of oil and gas companies were forced to let some of their senior staff go. In this case, severance packages up to a year or more in remuneration would have been paid out. This payout usually happens all at once, draining cash from the business quickly and in large amounts. If a company is not ready for it, it can be devastating to the organization.

In this section, we've discussed several items that can potentially expose your business to cash losses. Every business has contractual obligations that commit you to cash payouts into the future, and some that commit you to reconciling unknown amounts of cash.

You can't predict everything that might impact your business, but, as a business owner, you *can* put the effort into understanding all your contracts. Consider them carefully before you enter into them and be aware of the exposure risks that apply.

PROFIT VERSUS CASH

Do you know the difference between *profit* and *cash?*

Many business owners get these two terms mixed up, or they use them interchangeably. In this section of the book, we will discuss the difference between profit and cash and explain why this difference is important to understand.

Cash Is What You Have Today

The term *cash* represents the cash you actually have on hand today. This includes everything in your cash accounts as well as those items that can be turned quickly into cash.

These items include:

- Accounts receivable
- Bonds
- Guaranteed Investment Certificates (GICs)
- Short-term investments

The cash that your business has today has come from the three sources we mentioned above: operating, financing, and investing. Cash is a dollar amount frozen in time, and it is easily measurable and quantifiable. At that moment in time, either you have it or you don't. End of story.

Profit Is Your Future Cash

Profit, in contrast, is the difference between the amount you invest in your product and the amount you make from your product. Profit is not the same as cash, but they are related; profit reflects your ability to generate cash in the future.

Profit only flows from one of the three main divisions of your business listed above — the operations. Simply put, it comes from selling a product or service to a third party at a cost greater than what it cost you to provide that product or service.

Many business owners use the terms *profit* and *cash* interchangeably or get them confused. A business can have lots of cash in its bank account, but a combination of low profit, bad investments, and a lack of financing can cause your business to experience a cash shortage in no time flat. Conversely, a company with no cash but a profitable business can find itself closing its doors due only to its cash situation.

You probably know how much cash you have, but how do you know what your business profit is?

The paperwork you receive periodically from your staff may include profit and loss statements as well as cash flow statements. Studying these documents can give you valuable information; they can help you understand the current state of your business and help you to make informed decisions about the future.

When you're looking at the health of your business, which is more important—profit or cash?

How do you determine what to watch out for and when?

The answer is: They are both important. You need to keep your eyes and ears peeled watching both cash and profit at the same time, and this can be a challenge.

The Need to Consider Cash Flow and Profit Simultaneously: An Example

An example of how difficult this concept is for a business owner can be explained by telling you about a recent conversation I had with someone who had been in business for more than five years. His company was working on a large project that was about a third of the way under construction.

All the investment money for that project had been received upfront, and it had gone into a consolidated business operating account. Sales had been quite successful on the project, and when the project was completed — in nine months — they were anticipating a healthy return for the company.

When looking at the cash flow for the next nine months, however, the cash coming in was significantly less than the cash going out. There was revenue money to be recognized, and there was the cost of building the product; but the investment money, plus the share of returns for the investors, also had to be taken into consideration.

If we were looking at the project in isolation for the full twelve months, then the profit from the project would equal the positive cash flow from that job. But, because they were a third of the way through, and the investor money had already come in, the next nine months of cash flow would be negative because money would be paid out to the investors again.

This was a difficult concept for the owner to grasp because, in his mind, his calculations were always made using an equation like this:

If I sell the project for this much – A – and it cost me this much – B – then when the project closes in nine months, I should have A minus B in my cash bank account.

This is totally the wrong way of thinking. This business owner was only considering the theoretical profit, and not the actual flow of cash.

Having the Right Balance between Cash and Profit

What is the right balance between having cash on hand and using that cash in order to generate future business profit?

This is a critical question, and it requires an in-depth understanding of your business and its specific operations. You don't want too much money lying around, not doing anything for you, and you certainly don't want to be faced with a shortage of cash when you least expect it. This is where a forecast—a cash flow report—can come in handy.

I would recommend a detailed three-month cash flow statement as well as a high-level three-year cash flow statement. Unfortunately, as mentioned before, these reports are not provided by most small business accounting software. In addition, most bookkeepers and intermediate accountants don't have the expertise or the in-depth understanding of your business required to assemble this kind of report.

Remember, the cash flow of your company involves the many ins and outs of operating activities, financing activities, and investing activities. To run a comprehensive cash flow statement, you need to be aware of all these transactions.

CHAPTER TWO EXERCISES

- What transactions in your business are currently providing you with cash?

- What areas of your business are draining your cash? What can you do to improve this?

- Who owes you money, but hasn't paid you in a while?

- Do you have a loan schedule, detailing all your outstanding loans and their maturity dates?

- Do you know when your loan advances will happen and what you need to do to obtain them?

- Will you need to make any large purchases in the near future? Is financing an option for you?

- Is any business money sitting idle on a regular basis?

- What contracts do you have that can leave your business exposed to future cash drains?

- What is the right balance of profit and cash in your business?

CHAPTER THREE

Why Are You Hemorrhaging Cash, and How Can You Improve?

HOW MOST BUSINESSES LOSE MONEY

In order to be an empowered and successful business owner, you need to understand both cash and profit, as we've already discussed. Knowing the common pitfalls for small businesses is a crucial part of this process.

There are three areas most likely to cause financial challenges for a small business:

- Sales
- Operations
- Finance

Let's discuss each of them in more detail.

Sales

Your sales team is in charge of the front end of your business, which involves:

- Branding
- Marketing
- Customer relations
- Sales pricing
- Closing sales
- Social media
- Advertising

Without the sales department, your business would probably have no sales, and without sales, you would have no business. Depending on the size of your company, you may be doing all the sales work yourself, or you may employ several people to do it for you. Either way, attention needs to be given to each part of the sales process.

Knowing how to reach and attract your customers in an effective manner is critical to your success. You have a product to sell, but you need to ensure that your customers will buy it. Having a product of good quality at a good price is a start, but appropriate sales techniques are also required to sell products well. You need to make your product attractive to the customer, so they will want to buy from you, instead of buying from your competitor.

It is essential that you set up the sales part of your business properly and manage it well. The sales process funnels directly into the other two areas—operations and finance—so if you get it wrong, it can have far-reaching consequences. Hiring the right people for each part of the process is the first step. Most small business owners need to seek others to provide expert services in various areas, but there are many service providers available, and it can be very confusing.

When I was developing what my own business looked like—what I was selling, what my brand stood for, who I could best serve—and I had the opportunity to consult with several experts in their fields. For example, I consulted with a branding expert, a public speaking expert, a social media expert, and a consulting coach.

Instead of selecting experts in each strategically important field, most small business owners end up going with an all-in-one service, which is often a mistake. Using your website designer as your branding expert, social media expert, and marketing consultant is probably not a good idea. Each of these jobs requires a different skillset. If you choose your providers unwisely, you could end up spending more later.

Don't rush this process. It can take some time to research and hire the right providers. After that, it takes more time to work with the experts to develop the best approach for your business. For example, the process I went through to develop my company brand with my branding expert took almost six months of in-depth analysis.

Some of the branding details I had to figure out are listed below:

- The services I would offer
- The values I stood for
- The design of my customer avatar
- The language I would use to attract a customer
- Color selection
- Font style
- Graphics design

One of the dangers of not getting the details right is, after putting time, money, and effort into a product launch, you could find that you're attracting customers you don't want—or worse—you're not attracting customers at all. The cost to redo the work can really add up.

Within the sales framework of your business, many areas could be susceptible to loss of money or wasteful spending. Make sure that you are working with qualified individuals who are experts in their field. If you don't, you'll put everything you've worked for at risk. You may save money in the short term, but could end up paying more in the end.

Operations

The operations department is the department that makes things happen, and if you happen to be selling a product, it is likely where most of your costs are incurred. This part of your business needs constant and close monitoring when it comes to money and profit. In operations, areas to watch out for are numerous.

Some examples are:

- Wastage
- Production inefficiencies
- Service costs
- Labor costs
- Material costs
- Storage
- Inventory theft
- Spoilage

Usually your operations team is one of the largest departments within your organization. If you provide a service rather than a physical product, service cost can become a significant drain on your cash resources, and it needs to be monitored very closely. Don't forget to factor in your time as well.

The sum of the costs associated with delivering a product or service is referred to as the *cost of sales*. Each industry has its unique *expense to revenue ratio* — this is the cost of sales as a percentage of actual sales.

As a business owner, it is imperative that you know your cost of sales percentage compared with that of your competitors.

For a new product, an accurate calculation can only be made by meticulously assessing your projected costs and revenue. Once you know what your percentage should be, you can gauge where your business is in relation to that target and start doing something about it. Tracking and monitoring it on a monthly basis is strongly recommended.

Business Costs: An Example of Poor Planning

A great example of how cost of sales can send your business into a cash tailspin is in the story of a company I was asked to help not long ago.

This company was building a mixed-use condominium project, but they had never built one of this magnitude or scope. They had a vision of what it would look like, but did not fully take into consideration what it would take to build. The concept was a young, trendy, loft product with lots of jut-outs, flat roof systems, and color splashes. They hoped this would sell to the new, up-and-coming inner-city demographic.

The project plan focused too much on the sales side of things and too little on projecting the costs. The project moved forward based on an average square-foot consumption, which was completely inadequate. Costs were not vetted through a tendering process, which cost the company even more money.

The length of time to build the project turned out to be more than double the estimates. This added additional financing costs, additional labor costs, and overages pertaining to the basic scope of the work. At the project's end, rather than making a 10 percent return on investment, which is standard for their industry, the company lost 10 percent. Being their first big project, this loss was instrumental in the draining of both cash and profit out of the business. It will take years for this business to dig itself out of this hole.

Finance

The third and last department of your business that you must keep a close watch over is the finance department. This department is usually led by a vice president of finance or by a CFO in larger organizations. For a smaller business, it may be led by a controller, an accountant, or possibly a bookkeeper alone.

Within this department, there are often several sub-departments, like:

- Accounting
- Overhead
- Human resources (HR)
- Information technology (IT)
- Bank/lender financing

Let's look at the costs incurred by the finance department. When most business owners think about costs in general, they usually think about the costs associated with overhead, and they are significant.

Overhead costs include such things as:

- Payroll
- Rent
- Insurance
- Travel
- Consulting
- Office costs
- Group benefits
- Vacation costs
- Software upgrades
- Licensing
- Interest on loans
- Costs related to unproductive work by your staff

These costs can be small when looked at individually, but add them together, and they become significant.

Without a proper understanding of what these costs are and should be, money could be slipping through your fingers without you even knowing it. Most business owners view these costs as a necessary evil and don't spend the time to develop a proactive approach for keeping the costs under control.

If I were to draw a parallel example of this to your personal life, how many of us really spend the time to track and analyze what we spend each month as individuals?

We usually wait until the credit card bill comes in, and then we are faced with the sticker shock. Most of us will make an internal commitment to do better next month, but we usually never do.

Why is this?

It's because we tend to get caught up in the moment. We see something we like, and then we buy it. The cost of that thing we just bought goes out of sight, and out of mind. We lack the personal discipline to do anything about it. Part of getting control of the costs of your business is understanding why this undisciplined spending happens at all. Gaining the knowledge of what the costs are, and then doing something about it, is key to your profit and cash management.

WHY DOES IT HAPPEN?

In this section, we are going to look at why companies struggle to keep their costs under control. We are going to focus on the common factors that play a part in a company's lack of discipline. Once we have them identified, we can move on to some solutions that empower you, as a business owner, to take control of those costs.

Lack of Budgets for Sales and Overhead

One of the most common reasons that most businesses don't have control of their costs is that they don't budget for them in the first place.

How can you hold yourself accountable to your business spending if you don't even have a budget to refer to?

As I said before, your sales and marketing department play a large role in the cost and profit that run through your business. This is why sales and marketing budgets are critical.

For each product, you should have a detailed budget for your sales department that provides information such as:

- Quantity
- Selling price
- Incentive costs
- Timing of sales
- Loss leaders
- Promos

You should also have a detailed budget regarding the costs of production as well. It should include:

- Labor
- Material
- Subcontract services
- Storage
- Delivery
- Financing costs
- Insurance costs

It is critical for you to understand the cash flow issues involved with your products. Accordingly, establish a calendar that clearly shows the time differential for costs and payments. In this way, you can plan for the impact that your projects will have on your cash balance over time. On your calendar, you will clearly mark when each of the costs will need to be paid, and you will mark when money is expected to come in for each sale.

You will have to build a marketing plan before you can put any marketing budget in place — so that you know what to budget for.

Your plan might include:

- Website design
- Radio or television advertising
- Signage
- Magazine articles
- Product launches

Each of these marketing strategies will have a monetary cost. When you establish a marketing plan and put together a detailed marketing budget, you will be able to be proactive about planning for cash disbursements *before* the bills start to come in.

When you review your final budget, you will have the chance to alter your marketing plan based on cost-controlling initiatives. If you don't go through this process, more than likely you will spend the money first, and ask yourself for forgiveness later.

Your overhead budget should be calculated in the same way. For budgeting overhead costs, start with fixed costs that are nonnegotiable, such as rent, licensing, and business insurance. Then, gradually work in those items that are variable in nature, such as salaries, travel, entertainment, and office supplies.

Just as your marketing budget requires a marketing plan, your overhead budget requires a plan. You'll need to determine the parameters of your total overhead budget, and to come up with appropriate numbers, you will need to consider all the major factors that may have an impact on your particular business.

When determining the right total dollar value to allocate to overhead, consider doing a bit of research about what your competitors spend, how old your business is and whether you are downsizing or expanding for next year. A ratio of total overhead costs to sales revenue is a good metric to use. For the home building industry, an overhead percentage as it relates to sales dollars is standard between 5 and 7 percent.

For example:

- Is your business facing start-up costs?

- Is your business downsizing?

- Are you getting ready to ramp up for next year?

- Are you developing a new product that requires research and development dollars?

- Are you implementing a new software program that will require significant resources?

Your business planning process should be started about three months before year-end. A good business plan will take four to six weeks to develop for the upcoming year. Once your business plan is complete, your sales, marketing, and overhead budgets can be assembled. Usually a minimum of two versions of each budget will be required. To compile a more accurate budget, the vetting process usually takes more than one run-through.

First, each overhead budget item is given separate focus and assigned a value. Then, the consolidated budget is totaled. It is usually reviewed at a higher management level. More often than not, it is pushed back down the chain with budget cuts and reallocations based on company priorities. Depending on the size of the organization, this process may repeat another one or two times before final sign-off of the budget, so this process will take at least another four to six weeks.

Not the Right Reports

One other reason many businesses don't adequately control their costs is simply because the owners don't have timely access to the right reports.

I strongly believe that reporting is key to the success of any business.

We've already discussed the difference between historical, current, and future reporting. Right now, I am referring to current reporting.

What is going on in your business right now?

Is anything happening that, if acknowledged and acted on, could change the future success of your business?

Here are some examples:

- If you knew the labor component of a product you sell just rose by 2 percent over the last month, would you act on this in some way?

- If you knew that your vehicle costs for this month almost doubled from what it has typically been in the past, would you check into the possibility that the company truck is being used for personal reasons?

- If your payroll costs just went up without explanation, would you check into the possibility that employees clocked in unauthorized overtime?

It's essential that pertinent information get into your hands as quickly as possible so you have the chance to do something about it. There are several reports that can help you get a look at these costs before they get out of hand.

In addition to your regular bookkeeping reports and statements, there are three monthly reports that you want to be sure you have prepared and featured on your dashboard:

- An overhead variance report
- A project variance report
- A key performance indicators (KPI) report

An overhead variance report compares the actual costs for the current month to the costs you budgeted for that month. This will give you an indication of whether you are on track toward your goals.

A variance report cross-references current costs with past trends. When compared to your normal state of business, this type of report can give you an indication of whether your costs have changed.

Your key performance indicators (KPI) report should be prepared on a monthly basis, but should be tied in to your year-to-date numbers. To set up this report, you, as the owner, need to select which strategic indicators are of the highest importance to your business. Your key personnel will help you establish these items as part of the business planning process.

Then, each month, the KPI report will highlight for you these particular aspects of your business, letting you know their status.

Some common indicators are:

- Timelines
- Overtime hours
- Customer ratings
- Employee turnover
- Profit margins
- Inventory levels

Blending Personal Expenses with Business

Do you ever blend your personal expenses with the expenses of the business?

Do you assume that, because you own the business, it isn't necessary to keep the expenses separate?

This is an extremely common pitfall, and it can create significant cost-control challenges for a small business. This challenge often results from a lack of discipline over the use of company-issued credit cards.

I hear comments like these all the time:

What's the difference if I use the company credit card for personal items?

Why can't I use my personal credit card sometimes to pay for company business?

In the end, all the expenses come out of my pocket, so it really doesn't matter, does it?

This couldn't be further from the truth. Besides the fact that it is poor business practice, this lack of discipline makes it difficult for the accounting staff to do their jobs. They can't produce accurate reports if business expenses are mixed with personal expenses.

The success of your business contributes to your overall personal success, but it needs to be monitored and kept separate at all times. I am not saying that you, as an owner, can't have personal money flowing in and out of your business. That is to be expected, but this money should be handled through an account called your *shareholders' loan account.*

If an expense is a business expense, use the corporate credit card or pay for it with a check out of the business checking account. If it is a personal expense, then use your own personal money or your personal credit card to pay that expense. Simply follow that rule, and your business and personal accounts can stay intact and be used to track and measure performance accurately.

What about travel costs?

Business owners often struggle with establishing whether a travel expense is personal or business-related for tax return purposes.

When you are looking to deduct a travel expense, ask yourself these kinds of questions:

- Do you have documentation that clearly shows that the reason for traveling is business related?

- If you attended a meeting, do you have a set agenda for the meetings attended, including minutes and action items?

- If you traveled to gain product knowledge or to establish business relationships, do you have clear physical evidence of this?

No?

Then it is not a legitimate business travel expense. Your business is always at risk for being audited, and travel is one area that the taxman likes to investigate very closely. My recommendation for you is to document, document, and then document.

THE PROFIT MODEL

Now we are getting into the exciting part of the book, in which I will start to give you some tools to make your business more profitable, and to improve its overall cash position and health. You will be learning about my *three-dimensional profit model.* I will explain the main components below and I will show you its three-dimensional nature in the next chapter.

The Profit Formula

When you think about profit in your business, what comes to mind?

Making more than you spend?

Having money left over at the end of the day?

Profit is simply a mathematical formula for a desired outcome. It is made up of six key components and only these six components can affect how much profit you make.

The six components of the formula for profit are as follows:

1. The number of leads that come in to your business
2. Your ability to convert those leads into actual sales
3. The average sale price of your product or service
4. Your cost for providing that product or service
5. The overhead cost to keep your business running
6. The amount of taxes you pay to the taxman

Nothing else matters when it comes to calculating your profit. Let's use a simple example to demonstrate this.

Sheldon's Sweaters: Planning by Using the Profit Formula

Sheldon is a sweater manufacturer. He manufactures and sells wool sweaters for a reason—Sheldon wants to make one hundred dollars at the end of the day to support his family.

I've given you the six components of the profit formula in the list above. Let's calculate Sheldon's current profit formula. To do this, we will work backwards through the list, starting with taxes.

Sheldon's current profit formula:

6. *Taxman*: Sheldon wants to make $100 every day, and he knows he will pay 40 percent of what he makes to the taxman; therefore, his net profit before taxes is $166.67.

5. *Overhead*: Sheldon's overhead cost each day to run the office and to keep the lights on in the barn is $200, so his gross profit must be $366.67.

4. *Production costs*: Sheldon knows the cost of producing the sweaters, including shearing the sheep, spinning the yarn, and knitting the sweater, must be 85 percent of what he can sell them for. Doing the math, this is $2077.80. So, his sales total for the day needs to be $2,44.47.

Here's the check: $2444.47 minus $2077.80 gives you the $366.67 net profit.

3. *Sale Price*: Sheldon can sell his sweaters for $150 each.

2. *Conversion of Leads*: He needs to sell at least seventeen sweaters a day to meet his sales goal.

1. *Number of Leads*: One out of every four customers who walks into Sheldon's store buys a sweater, so he needs sixty-five customers walking through his door every day.

Now Sheldon has identified the six key profit measurements that make a difference in his business.

See the chart below:

Sheldon's Current Daily Profit Number		$100.00
His current tax rate	(6)	40%
Required Net Profit Before Tax	(100/(1-0.4))	$166.67
Current Overhead Costs	(5)	$200
Required Gross Profit to Cover Overhead	(166.67 + 200)	$366.67
Current Cost of Sales	(4)	85%
Required Revenue or Sales to Support Sheldon's Business	(366.67/ (1-0.85))	$2,444.47
Average Sale Price of Each Sweater	(3)	$150.00

Number of Sweaters Sheldon is Required to Sell	(2,444.47/ 150)	16.30
Conversion Rate (1 out of 4)	(2)	25%
Number of Walk-in Customers Needed (16.30/0.25)	(1)	65.19

Using the Profit Formula to Plan for Improvements

Now that Sheldon knows each of these components, what if he made some slight adjustments?

What if he focused on improving each area by only 5 percent?

At a 5 percent improvement:

- The number of people who walk into his store improves from 65 to 69.

- His conversion rate changes from 25 percent to 26.25 percent.

- His average sales go up from $150 to $157 dollars.

- His cost of sales goes down to 80 percent from 85.

- He reduces his overhead by $10 a day, and now it sits at $190.

- He manages to utilize some tax-saving advice and now pays 35 percent versus 40 percent.

What is his take-home pay at the end of the day?

That's right. He now takes home $244 versus $100 per day. That is almost two and a half times what he was making before.

See the chart below:

Sheldon's Improved Daily Profit Number		$244.44	5% improvement to each of the 6 profit drivers
His improved tax rate	(6)	35%	Got advice from his tax accountant
Required Net Profit Before Tax (566.06 - 190)		$376.06	
Reduced Overhead Costs	(5)	190	Save on heating costs of the barn
Required Gross Profit to Cover Overhead (2830.28 x (1-0.80))		$566.06	

Reduced Cost of Sales	(4)	80%	Found a more efficient spinning wheel
Required Revenue or Sales to Support Sheldon's Business (17.97 x 157.50)		$2,830.28	
Improved Sale Price of Each Sweater	(3)	$157.50	Added patterns to the sweaters
Number of Sweaters Sheldon Can Now Sell (68.45 x 0.2625)		17.97	
Improved Conversion Rate	(2)	26.25%	Tweaked his closing pitch
Increased Walk-ins in Sheldon's Store	(1)	68.45	Started using social media

In the chart, you can also see how Sheldon has planned to improve each area by 5 percent, starting with getting advice from his tax accountant.

Envision Sheldon going to trusted members of his team to ask for advice. When opening a discussion with team members, he could do it with pinpoint focus — on just one of the six components of profit at a time. This would have made brainstorming with his team easier, faster, and more effective.

How difficult do you think it was for Sheldon and his team to come up with simple strategies to get him 5 percent improvement?

The Six Foundations of Business

Now let's look at the six foundations of your business and learn how you can focus your attention to develop these key strategies. To stay on top of your company's success, you need to ensure that all six of these cylinders are firing. We will discuss each of them.

They are as follows:

1. Sales maximization
2. Operational excellence
3. Customer satisfaction
4. Employee engagement
5. Financial success
6. Research and development

Sales Maximization

Your sales team needs to be driving leads, finding better ways to convert them to sales, finding ways to upsell and serve your customers, raising your average selling price, or increasing the number of times your customer buys from you.

Operational Excellence

Your operations team should always be looking for better ways to build your product, reduce time frames, find better quality materials, avoid service or recall challenges, and reduce material costs. Small changes can improve profit significantly. In the case above, notice that just by moving from 85 percent cost to 80 percent cost made a huge impact on the success of Sheldon's business.

Customer Satisfaction

Customer satisfaction is also a large contributor to word-of-mouth advertising, referrals, and repeat business. Spending some devoted time and energy in this area is also key to your business success.

What is your current customer satisfaction rating?

If you don't know, I would suggest researching a third-party audit survey to find out.

Keep in mind: *You can't manage what you don't measure.*

Remember this idea; it will come in handy in many areas of your business.

Employee Engagement

Employee engagement is one area that is always overlooked. Owners think that if no one is speaking up, then everything must be going okay. They may be speaking up, but not to you. This is why you need a strong HR presence within your company.

Consider these HR questions:

- Do you have clear job descriptions or roles clearly defined with set expectations?
- Are performance reviews done on a regular basis?
- Are the right people in the right roles?
- Are employees currently being challenged?

Very few companies, if any, have employees who are 100 percent engaged 100 percent of the time. It is possible that unproductive time is rampant in your business. It is your responsibility to keep it to a minimum.

Financial Success

- What do we mean by financial success?

- For the purpose of our discussion, it is *financial discipline.*

- Accordingly, financial success for your business means:

- Money is not wasted for nonproductive purposes.

- Everyone in the business is focused on how they individually contribute to profit.

- Your business is strategically aligned with lending partners who can see you through the good times and the bad.

- You are prepared for the future regarding tax planning and growth.

- You are looking internally within your company for roadblocks and opportunities, as well as externally.

Research and Development

The sixth and last foundation that forms a pillar for your business is research and development. If you are not improving, then you are falling behind. You can rest assured that your competitors are consistently striving to be better tomorrow than they were yesterday.

You can look at technology to see many obvious examples.

How many times do we see the newest phone come out with more bells and whistles than last year's model?

Marketing has moved away from old-school ways and is starting to flourish on social media. Online shopping with drones that deliver to your door, cars that drive themselves — this is the way of our future. If you don't stay on top of it, you are going to be left behind. Every business owner should invest in, and dedicate time and energy to, staying ahead of the marketplace.

Taking Action

Where do you go from here?

You now know the profit formula, and you are aware of the six foundational pillars in your business.

What do you do with your information?

I am sure, after reading the last two sections of this chapter, your mind is spinning a bit. Maybe some quick thoughts jumped into your head and then just as quickly they left. That is the challenge with most entrepreneurs — you are a creative person, often with many simultaneous thoughts and ideas.

How do you capture them all?

We will talk more about this later in the book.

What I want to mention here is that it's important to take action. With everything you have on your plate as an owner, it is tough to take more on. However, the action you're contemplating may be an important one. It could be that if you get this right, the rest of your business will start to operate smoothly.

I also want to mention that this takes a certain amount of discipline and training. I don't know how many businesses I have seen in my past in which the management has gone through the motions of formulating a solid plan of action, only to lose focus along the way.

It's human nature. We make a New Year's resolution, and six weeks into it, we drop it. We start a new diet, and then we give in to temptation and go back to our old ways. We attend a conference, come back with two or three strategic game-changers, get our team on board, and before you know it, we don't even remember what those game-changers were.

What I want to emphasize here is that you are in charge of your own destiny. You are either going to make it happen, or you are not. You are either going to put the time and effort in, or you won't. It's up to you. It's time for the rubber to meet the road.

CHAPTER THREE EXERCISES

- Spend some time completing your current organizational chart.

- Who is looking after your sales, your operations, and the financial side of your business? Make sure to include all the subdepartments as well.

- Label yourself in all areas of the chart that you are currently responsible for, then take a step back and look at it. What do you see?

- Who, in your circle, pushes you to be creative and move forward?

- How much time do you spend planning and working *on* your business versus working *in* it?

- Do you have a business plan and a marketing plan? Do you have budgets to support them?

- Remember what I said about not being able to manage what you don't measure? In order for you to use the profit formula, you need to track and measure the six components:

  Do you track your leads?
  How many of them convert?
  Do you know your average selling price?
  Do you know your cost of sales percentage?

Do you have a handle on what your overhead costs are?

How much do you pay the taxman?

- What items could you improve by 5 percent to advance your profit formula?

- Are you ready to commit to making a difference going forward?

CHAPTER FOUR

How Can You Prepare, and What Tools Do You Need?

ASSESS YOUR CURRENT STATE OF AFFAIRS

You are ready to take action now, to begin your journey on the road to success. Before you can set off, you will need to gather some information and make some plans.

Staying with this metaphor, consider the following questions:

- What kind of car are you driving?
- How fast can it go?
- What types of cars are your competitors driving?
- What lane are they in compared to you?
- What road construction is up ahead that might impede your passage?
- How do you prepare for this journey?

Before you can act and set the wheels in motion to bring you toward success, you must first figure out where you are in relation to where you want to go.

113

Only then can you begin to develop your roadmap to profit. These are some of the key concepts we will be discussing in this chapter.

The SWOT Analysis

Most business people are familiar with the SWOT analysis, but if you aren't, it simply stands for the process of analyzing these four areas of your business:

- **S**trengths
- **W**eaknesses
- **O**pportunities
- **T**hreats

Strengths and *weaknesses* refer to those items that are internal for your organization; *opportunities* and *threats* relate to those items that are external to your organization.

Most businesses will complete a SWOT analysis as the key component of their strategic planning. It seems logical that *profit* should be the key focus of strategic planning instead, but, remarkably, it is often the component left out!

My model for strategic planning has been developed in a different way from the usual pattern for planning. We begin with a simplified version of a typical SWOT analysis, but we will organize it into a matrix that relates to the profit formula and the six foundations of business previously mentioned.

The concept has these benefits:

- It is easy to understand.

- It focuses on profitability, which we have determined as being critical to your business's success.

- It drives performance throughout all areas of your business.

- It takes the process one step further, adding positive and proactive action.

Create Your Strategic Planning Grid

Here's how it works:

First, take the six components of the profit formula — leads, conversion rate, average selling price, cost of sales, overhead, and taxes — and create a column for each across the top of your page.

Next, take the six foundations of business — sales maximization, operational excellence, customer satisfaction, employee engagement, financial discipline, and research and development — and create a row for each across the left-hand side of the page.

This will form a six-by-six grid, where each profit component cross-sections with the six key business foundations, thereby creating a two-dimensional strategic planning grid.

See the chart below:

	Leads	Conversion Rate	Avg Price	Cost of Sales	Over-head Cost	Tax Rate
Sales Maximization	*	*	*	*	*	*
Operational Excellence	*	*	*	*	*	*
Customer Satisfaction	*	*	*	*	*	*
Employee Engagement	*	*	*	*	*	*
Financial Dicipline	*	*	*	*	*	*
Research & Development	*	*	*	*	*	*
* Identify roadblocks and opportunities in each cross section						

Identify Opportunities and Roadblocks

In the planning process, your goal for each grid section is to identify opportunities and roadblocks for that particular section. These opportunities and roadblocks could be internal or external, current or future.

Take some time to look over the grid and consider how each component of the profit formula interacts with each foundation of business. Ask yourself questions about the relationships. Take notes on opportunities and challenges.

For example:

- How does the focus of sales maximization affect lead conversion?

- How does customer satisfaction relate to cost of sales?

- How does financial discipline affect overhead?

- What opportunities are you seeing in your business in these cross-sections?

- What roadblocks need to be removed?

The Third Dimension

The third dimensional aspect of my model is a way in which you can maximize your results.

Think of a regular graph with an x-axis and a y-axis.

See the graph below:

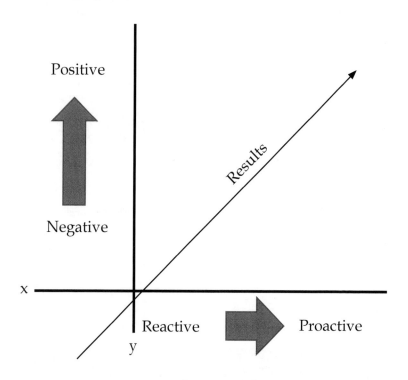

The x-axis is the bottom line. Picture that it shows your approach to problem solving, ranging from *reactive* to *proactive* as you move from left to right.

The y-axis is the vertical line and it shows your state of thinking. As you move upward on the y-axis, you move from a *negative* state of thinking to a *positive* state.

Now draw a diagonal line at 45 degrees from the bottom left to the top right. This is your *results* line.

How do you maximize your results?

The more positive you are, and the more proactive your approach is, the greater your results will be.

Putting All the Dimensions Together

Go back to your two-dimensional six-by-six grid above. After completing the exercise, you will have identified several key roadblocks and opportunities in your business, but it means nothing unless you do something with it. Bring that six-by-six grid out toward you, now creating a virtual cube, so to speak, where this third dimension is represented by positive, proactive action.

See the diagram below:

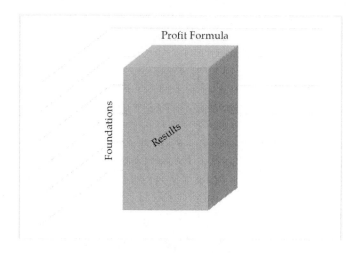

This three-dimensional diagram helps to accent this important concept: Without the key element of *action*, any strategic plan will be left flat, and will have little value to a business.

Planning for Action

Now, we all know that organization is the key to getting things done. To be organized, you should take time to prioritize what you have on your plate.

If you did your due diligence in the exercise above, it should have taken at least a few days and involved consultations with others, and you should now have a massive list of roadblocks to remove and challenges to overcome.

Next, you will select which of these items to act on, and create an action plan. Remember, without action, your strategic plan is useless.

Let's go back to our example of Sheldon and his sweater-making business and fill in a few grid sections.

Sheldon's Sweaters: Employee Engagement and Cost of Sales

How can employee engagement affect cost of sales?

Sheldon's production staff could potentially reduce his cost of sales by introducing a bonus plan or an incentive for additional time off. They could come up with a way to handle the sheep more efficiently during shearing time. This will reduce the amount of time it takes and therefore reduce the number of hours of labor required. If they reduce production time, they can reduce costs.

Sheldon's Sweaters: Research and Development and Selling Price

How can research and development impact the average selling price?

Sheldon could add a variety of dye lots to the production assembly line, creating the option for color patterns and designs on each of the sweaters, bringing their new selling price from $150.00 to $157.50 each.

So, you see where I am going with this. For each selected opportunity or roadblock, you will plan an appropriate action. Spend some time with your list and brainstorm some action plans to get comfortable with the idea.

Timing: Prioritize Your Strategies

You have now identified several opportunities to make beneficial changes, and have brainstormed some action plans.

Which do you implement first?

Knowing that they all take time, resources, and money, you must choose wisely. This is where your own discretion comes into play.

There are many issues to consider, and a few of them are:

- Timing: Some changes will have to be instigated before others simply from a process point of view.

- Revenue schedule: Some changes will be low-hanging fruit that can generate profit faster than others.

- Costs: Some changes will cost you money before they start generating you a return on investment, and you must be ready for those costs.

- Resources: Some changes will require resources that you don't already possess.

This is where it becomes important to get your plan right. A lot of companies, when going through a strategic planning session, invest in hiring a third party who specializes in this process and can keep everyone on track.

For this particular plan, because it relates to profit, I would recommend hiring a profit coach whose skill set is different from that of a business coach. I will explain in more detail in the next chapter.

Determine the Resources Required

As mentioned above, each new strategy may require some additional resources — time, people, money, or materials — to carry it out. When developing your plan, build a resource list under each action item with an associated cost component.

Remember, this strategic model is different than most. Our goals and objectives here are directed at making a business more profitable.

Ask yourself when you are evaluating each action item: *What is the direct profit benefit that my company will get out of it?*

Tie each item back into your profit formula, and plug in the anticipated results.

Sheldon's Sweaters: Tying Changes Back Into the Profit Formula

For example, in Sheldon's company, consider the option of adding the dye lot technology. As we stated, this change would enable the company to charge $157.50 per sweater.

Are there any additional costs involved with this proposal?

Yes, the research and development work must be paid for, and in addition, the materials cost for the product will increase due to the purchase of the new dyes. Sheldon will need to assess the new materials cost for each lot of sweaters, and plug the new numbers back into the profit formula to make sure his plan is still worth pursuing.

Do your due diligence to determine if each of your action items still gives a greater profit number when you consider additional cost factors. If it does, then it makes sense to go ahead with it.

For some proposals, the specific costs won't be apparent, and you may not be able to see the immediate impact on your business. The objective in these cases is to make the best decision you can, based on the characteristics of your business and your own knowledge.

As you try each new action item, follow up by measuring and testing, continually using the key dashboard reports that I mentioned earlier in the book.

THINK SHORT TERM AND LONG TERM

When you come up with new action plans, identify whether they are short-term or long-term.

This will help you to:

- Prioritize your strategies
- Identify roadblocks and opportunities that are relevant
- Set an appropriate timeline
- Guide you in measuring success of action items

This Year's Plan

There are specific reasons why I am talking about this year's plan before I discuss your quarterly goals or your three-year plan.

- Most business owners naturally think about progress in one-year increments.

- Most of your business statements and financial plans are in terms of one-year periods.

- When you talk about where you need to be or how you need to get there, you probably think about your current financial year first.

Overall, because it is easier for business owners to visualize and grasp as a concept, we discuss the annual plan first. It will put the groundwork in place for other variations.

How did you do last year?

When setting your goals for this year, a great framework or reference is looking back at how you did during the previous year. Using your current profit and loss statement framework—that your accounting staff has already set up in your accounting software—you can easily extrapolate and extend it for another twelve months.

Here are some questions to ask:

- What were your sales like?
- What were your costs like?
- How many people worked for you?
- What areas of the business could use some work?

- How much did you take home at the end of the day?
- Was it enough?
- What would you like to take home this year?

For example, in the case of Sheldon, last year he took home an average of $100 a day. This year, with his newly established goals, he can take home $244 a day. This will help him grow the business the way he wants to and give him the financial freedom he is looking for in his personal life.

When establishing your one-year plan, think about your goals and the specific action items you have selected to focus on, but also think about how it all plays out in your financial plan. You must do your best to see your new one-year vision as clearly as possible, and make a good financial forecast. I will elaborate on what this means in the next section when I outline what a financial strategic plan is.

I advise you to make your one-year financial forecast plan a rolling one. What I mean by this is that once you finish your first quarter, you should extend your forecast out another quarter. In this way, you will always be giving yourself a one-year forecast into your future. This will enable you to be as proactive as possible; you can reflect and adapt, making corrective actions when necessary.

Your Quarterly Goals

In my years of experience, I have seen many strategic business plans fail.

What are the most common reasons for failure?

Many plans fail when they become too big, and are enacted too fast; they simply become unmanageable. Owners forget that most of these action items are delegated downward and those people who become responsible for their implementation still have their regular nine-to-five jobs to do. If expectations are unrealistic, and communication of goals is inadequate, eventually the strategic plan will come to a grinding halt.

Does this scenario seem familiar to you?

Chances are you have experienced it yourself. You can see that programs must be carefully planned to avoid this scenario. Don't set your business plans — and your employees — up for failure.

Set reasonable and appropriate goals. Remember, goals should always be SMART in nature:

- **S**pecific
- **M**easurable
- **A**chievable
- **R**ealistic
- **T**imely

Here are some other suggestions:

- Don't plan to do too much.

- Be realistic with your timelines.

- Take your one-year plan, break it into four quarters, and set realistic quarterly goals.

- Give each quarter its own focus with key strategies, action items, stakeholders, resources required, and due dates attached to them.

- Attach specific Key Performance Indicator (KPI) measurements to each quarterly goal.

- Each person who is listed as a key stakeholder in the program should have a set goal and a KPI measurement.

- The goals and KPI measurements should be tied to the stakeholders' individual performance reviews.

- Each quarter, review what you have and have not accomplished.

During your quarterly review, you will reevaluate your plan and make any necessary adjustments. Carry over those items that you still deem important, and keep the momentum going. Remember that forward momentum is what gets things done. Don't beat yourself up when goals are not fully met. Positive, proactive thinking will always get you to your goal faster.

Your Three-Year Plan

Now that you have your one-year plan and your quarterly goals established to get you there, it is time to start dreaming a little bit bigger. It's time to create a three-year plan.

Depending on the type of business you have, a multi-year plan can be essential. In the case of long-term projects such as oil and gas, construction, and land acquisitions, it is crucial to have a long-term plan. In some businesses, the fluctuation of the market, foreign exchange rates, and international regulations make it necessary to plan ahead a minimum of three years.

For some businesses, activities in each year may depend on what happened in the previous year. For example, to have sufficient inventory in years two and three, it may be necessary to acquire that inventory in year one. It may take time to arrange for contracts to supply materials and services, and you may require timely infusions of cash for purchasing. Without some advanced planning, some projects will certainly fail.

The crux of the lesson is: *You always need to be thinking of the future while you are working on the present.*

Let's bring the conversation back to cash and profitability, since they are the main topics of this book.

How does long-term planning affect profitability?

It can deeply affect profits. Without proper planning, including long-term, you can easily find yourself short of cash and not have enough for the projects you need, or hemorrhaging potential profits.

When you are planning for three years, employ the same profit and loss forecasting template that you used for your one year plan. Simply extend it to three years. If you keep the format consistent from one year to another, this will allow you to use formula drivers such as year-over-year percentage changes. It will also enable you to extrapolate trends that represent busier times of the year.

Maintain a detailed cash-flow plan, adjusting it as your projects develop over the years. Watch out for those costs that come into play once a year but can drain a significant amount of cash. For example, corporate tax payments are a cash item that often gets forgotten; the company is sent into a tailspin when, suddenly, the money comes due. Plan ahead for these large cash outlays—the ones you know are coming—and they won't be any problem.

DEVELOP A FINANCIAL STRATEGIC PLAN

Before we delve into the details of a financial strategic plan, we need to define some terms.

What is a *business plan?*

What is a *strategic plan?*

If you aren't sure of the difference, you're not alone.

Business Plan

A *business plan* is simply a written report that indicates the framework, goals, and logistics of running your business. Your business plan will be required when you seek investors, apply for business loans, and engage in other transactions.

A business plan usually contains the following sections:

- An overview of your business
- Crucial company details
- Personal goals
- Your business vision
- Business objectives
- Product overview
- Industry factors and trends
- Your competitive advantage
- Your competition at a glance
- Your customer avatar

- Sales and marketing plans
- Business operations tactics
- Teams, suppliers, and alliances
- Any changes from previous plans
- Any contingency plans
- Your personal finances
- Your business finances
- Cash flow projections

Strategic Plan

In contrast, a *strategic plan* details how your business should proceed in order to reach the goals you've set. It is an action plan.

All businesses will construct a detailed business plan. It is a basic requirement, as we've already stated, for business loans and other transactions. A strategic plan might not be required by any outside services at all.

Does every business have a strategic plan?

If you look back at the definition given above—an action plan for how you will proceed toward your goals—I think you will agree that all businesses must craft a strategic plan. However, it might look very different from company to company. A strategic plan could be relatively informal in some small businesses. In a business that is large or multifaceted, it could be a complex document.

A strategic plan should be carefully crafted for any business; if you want to reach your goals, creating action plans that support them is essential. In this section, we will look at the way a strategic plan is traditionally formulated, and discuss the shortcomings of this process. Then, we will look at my process for *financial strategic planning.*

If you are a business owner, you may be crafting your strategic plan yourself. As you read ahead, you will see that formulating a financial strategic plan involves a variety of factors that may be challenging to incorporate on your own. Hiring the right kind of business coach to lead you through your strategic planning can save you time and give you better results.

A Financial Strategic Plan Is Different From a Regular Strategic Plan

How does a financial strategic plan differ from a regular — common — strategic plan?

Let's discuss first how a regular strategic plan is typically constructed.

The process usually begins with an attempt to establish a baseline framework that describes who you are, which customers you want to serve, and where you want your business to be when it grows up. Typically, this will involve discussions with key personnel about your company's vision, mission, core values, and guiding principles.

Commonly, business owners will set aside some planning time for these discussions. In some companies, a two-day planning retreat is scheduled. Let's look at a strategic planning agenda, based on what I've experienced in the business world.

On the first day, the focus will be on conversations that are, for lack of a better word, *fluffy* — they are not results-driven conversations. Everyone in senior management will spend the day engaged in conversations about feelings, but no action will be taken.

In my roles over the years as vice president of finance and chief financial officer, I have had the opportunity to participate in numerous such meetings.

I am not discrediting this type of approach, but here is what I have come to understand about this process:

- It takes a great deal of time to go through this exercise.

- After having gone through it, participants often feel somewhat emotionally drained.

- As the day ends, most people have a sense that a big hurdle has been overcome, although this may not be the case at all.

- Employees typically start to get anxious after spending so many hours on this exercise; they want to get back to the work that is building up in the office.

On the second day of strategic planning, usually each department head commits to their individual goals and objectives for the year. The whole day is used to determine the key strategies that managers will be responsible for in the upcoming year. This activity is typically driven by doing a SWOT analysis, as mentioned earlier on in the book.

Here are my observations about this second part of the process:

- As I have mentioned before, a SWOT analysis is vague in nature; because of the lack of a distinct focal point, a wide variety of initiatives may be brought forward.

- These initiatives may make sense at the time, but do not necessarily relate back to profit. In fact, the value of many of these proposals may well end up being less than the cost it takes to put them into action.

- At the end of day two, most plans have the strategies in place, but very few have drilled down into the specific action items.

- I would say that fewer than half of the strategic planning sessions I have attended in my career ever shared their past year's financial performance with team leaders as a basis to try to determine what this year's goals are.

- KPIs are generally not reviewed and any reporting that is brought to these table meetings is basic at best.

- After this two-day process, the managers are expected to begin to implement strategies.

You Can't Manage What You Don't Measure

The organizers of these meetings certainly have access to important data that's been collected on the company's past performance, but you can see that this data is largely ignored. Overall, in my experience, the theme of these meetings tends to be to wipe the slate clean and start afresh.

The guiding statement I gave before applies here again: *You can't manage what you don't measure.*

If you don't stop to reflect where you have been, how do you know where you need to go?

If you don't review what's happened, how do you know what adjustments need to be made?

From this one strategic planning meeting, the managers will be instructed to take their individual strategies back to the office. They are then expected to put actions in place that will create results.

How do they know these actions are going to deliver profitable results?

Typically, there has been little investigation into the impact of the action plans on profit and cash. The managers are simply charged with getting the actions done. This is where the classic strategic plan starts to fall apart, even before it has begun.

How can we improve this process?

Characteristics of a Financial Strategic Plan

The answer is to revise the common strategic plan into a *financial* strategic plan, in which all financial considerations are taken into account.

For a financial strategic plan, questions like these are answered:

- How much time does each part of the plan take?
- What does it cost to finance the plan?
- What resources are required?
- How does the cost of the plan compare to the potential profit?

During the crafting of a financial strategic plan, every action item of the plan is reviewed to determine cost and resources required. Before committing to the action plan, the total cost of the plan is always calculated and measured against the potential additional profit it could generate.

Some other important tasks involved with financial strategic planning:

- Detailed department budgets should be completed, including sales, cost of sales, marketing, and overhead.

- A forecast of cash flow should be generated to support the plan.

- A projected balance sheet should be prepared to determine equity levels, cash levels, debt levels, and inventory levels to support the plan.

- An organizational chart should be developed.

- The responsibilities and remuneration for each position should be detailed.

- If new staff is added, the cost should be integrated into the plan.

- The information technology (IT) department should review the plan to determine hardware and software requirements and cost.

- The human resources (HR) department should be consulted to discuss group benefits and potential bonus plan initiatives.

This level of detail may surpass anything you've seen before in business. The strategic planning process is critical to business success, but, too often, it is given little attention.

Why?

Part of the reason is given by the title of this book: *Who Is Watching Your Money?*

There is a general lack of focus on money and profit in small businesses, which I've discussed in detail in the first chapter.

Another reason may be that the standard strategic planning model feels like a waste of time to business owners. Because it doesn't seem to produce much in the way of results, business owners don't put much energy into the process.

Change your model for strategic planning to the financial strategic planning model I've outlined here. It can make all the difference.

Timing of Financial Strategic Plans

The last topic that I want to discuss with you in this chapter is the timing of your strategic plan. Most business people start thinking about strategic planning for the next year as the current year is coming to a close. If you are crafting an annual strategic plan, this would correlate with month twelve of your current year.

This is about sixty days too late.

You need to start your strategic planning for your next year before the current year's third quarter ends. It will take sixty to ninety days to develop and roll out your plan.

Why do you need this much time?

- The financial strategic plan is extremely detailed, compared to standard plans.
- Many people must be involved in the process.
- Reports must be written and reviewed.
- Budgets must be created.
- The plan must be divided into individual action items, and assigned to your staff, with clearly outlined instructions.

Don't forget that the success of the plan requires the skillful implementation of that plan. The details must be rolled out in terms of individual action items for your staff. Communication of the details of the plan can be delivered at your town hall meetings or at an annual general meeting if you have one.

Besides formulating an annual plan, strategic planning may also be required any time there is a major shift in the business. In these cases, the strategic planning process should focus on those areas of the business that are in direct impact of the change, but, just like a regular strategic plan, the focus should be given to profitability using the three-dimensional profit model.

Here are some examples of times when a company might need to create a new strategic plan:

- The launch of a new division
- Changes in senior management
- A change in organizational structure
- A buy or sell arrangement

Strategic planning is not for the faint of heart; it requires discipline and coordination. It requires the strength of a great leader to ensure that the company stays on track, someone who can bring the team back on track if they start to deviate from the plan. If you get this right, then the rewards can be massive.

CHAPTER FOUR EXERCISES

- Complete your six-by-six profit grid as directed, and identify some opportunities and challenges that apply to your business. Complete this exercise with your team for best results.

- Develop some potential action strategies that relate to your selected roadblocks and opportunities. Don't select more than six to begin with. Choose strategies that really resonate with you, in areas where you think the best opportunities lie.

- Perform a sensitivity analysis to determine how each of your six strategies can generate more profit for your business. If it brings in more revenue than it costs to implement, then it has a positive impact on your future profit.

- Prioritize your strategies from the most impactful to the least impactful.

- Delegate your strategies to members on your team who can create and implement the action items.

- Organize the plan and all the correlating reports into one cohesive package so that everyone can have access, and it remains *ground zero* for future comparison purposes. Be sure to include cash flows, budgets, KPIs, and your forecasted profits and losses.

- Break down each action item into quarterly objectives to make it more manageable.

- Have your HR department include individual KPIs as part of each employee's performance review. The KPI evaluation result will affect the employee's performance review score. The performance review score can then be used to evaluate any profit sharing or bonus plan initiative that the company may have.

- Communicate the status of the plan and how it directly impacts their jobs and their deliverables with your staff. Review the plan monthly at leadership meetings. Above all else, hold yourself and your team accountable for delivering on the plan.

CHAPTER FIVE

Who Can Help You?

SHIFT YOUR OWN FOCUS

We have been talking about building your financial strategic plan to secure your future and about the necessity of shifting your focus forward toward cash and profitability.

Like every entrepreneur, you want to have a successful and profitable business, and you're willing to put in the work to attain it. We all know, however, that many businesses are unsuccessful, even when they have a quality product and highly qualified leaders.

Why do they fail?

There may be many reasons, but two common threads that often mark an unsuccessful business are:

- Failure to adequately focus on cash and profit
- Lack of financial strategic planning for the future

We have already discussed, at length, the importance of refocusing your attention on cash flow, and improving your planning process. There are other ways that you, as the business owner, can directly impact the efficiency and profitability of your company and we will discuss them in this chapter.

Implementing changes in your company can be challenging, and you may be feeling like you don't have the expertise to manage such adjustments successfully. However, you do not have to do it alone, and, in the pages that follow, we will talk about how to find experts to help you on your journey.

If You Don't Care, No One Else Will

You are the business owner, and as such, you are in the driver's seat. You will decide where your business is going. Your team is looking to you for guidance and inspiration. Your company's corporate culture is set by you.

Consider these questions:

- How do you behave when dealing with others?

- What language do you use when communicating with your staff?

- How do you hold them accountable for their deliverables?

- How do you motivate your employees to perform high-quality work?

People are not motivated to work hard so they can put money in your pocket. In order for cash management and profitability to be on everyone else's radar, they need to hear from you.

However, *how* you deliver your message is just as important as why you are delivering your message. As the business owner, you need to come at it from a position of *caring*.

Your behavior should demonstrate that you care about:

- Your customers
- Your team
- Being efficient and not wasting time
- The environment and not wasting material
- Being innovative with products and services you offer
- Celebrating the victories achieved so far

How well do you show that you care when you are communicating with your staff?

Think about it. Remember, your goal here is to create positive, proactive results.

Leadership: An Example of Speaking from the Heart

I had the pleasure of working for an individual who demonstrated a lot of passion as a leader. When he spoke to his team, he was always able to speak from the heart. In speaking this way, he was able to motivate his team to believe in his company's mission and purpose. He was not afraid to show his emotions in front of the team when the company struggled during hard times, and he also took the time to celebrate wins with his team as they happened. His attitude was inspiring and contagious.

This particular individual also happened to be great at measuring performance. He kept track of who was responsible for delivering results, and made them accountable for their responsibilities. He was able to tap in to the inner motivations of others and link their motivations to the success of the business.

Great leadership is vital to the success of a business.

Here are a few ways you might support your team members:

- Demonstrate for your employees how a profitable business can give your team job stability.

- Support the development of career ladders within your organizations and empower your team giving them enough flexibility to manage their staff professionally.

- Reward high-quality work. If possible, give your staff an opportunity to share in the company's profit, which in turn will help them achieve their own financial freedom.

People want to be a part of something special. As the business owner, think of your job as creating something special that is also profitable. Once it is profitable, you are responsible for maintaining its foundation and framework, supporting it so that it can be successful in the years to come.

Commit to Devoting Time and Resources

Making a business successful takes both time and resources. It doesn't just happen overnight. If you did try to change your business overnight, people would probably not buy into the process. They may get confused as to where this brand-new line of thinking is coming from and uncertain about how long it will last.

First, take stock of the amount of time and resources you are willing to commit to manage your cash properly and promote profitability within your organization.

We have already identified two key components regarding the resources you require:

1. You need the right people.
2. You need the right reports.

The right accounting team within your organization can provide you with knowledge. They can tell you how you are currently performing, and help you see where you need to go. Be sure to maximize the quality of your reports. Get rid of all the white noise in your business, and focus on those reports that will drive performance and create results.

Ensure you have the right people in the right roles. Hire people who have sound business minds and want to be part of something bigger than themselves. Fill your senior staff with people who can help you plan strategically for the future. Pull from resources outside of your business if you need to. Hire a consultant or seek expert advice during periods of growth or in times that are proving to be more challenging. Budget for these external resources as well, and plan to use them. They are a necessary investment for your business.

When faced with cash flow and profitability challenges, small business owners often cut spending in these areas — ceasing to allocate resources for staffing and planning. This is one of the worst things you can do to your business, but I have seen it happen time and time again. To cut spending, owners will often lay off members of their professional administrative staff — sometimes hiring a family member instead — and cancel events like their annual strategic planning retreat. This is narrow-minded thinking.

Instead of cutting back, you should be adding resources to support your investment.

Does this sound illogical?

To understand this proposal, consider why your business is having problems. In almost every case, you can trace the source of the problem to your management of staffing and planning.

Did the business economy shift and cause your business to suffer?

The reason you did not predict the changes in the economic environment that hurt your business is most likely because you didn't invest enough in your planning.

Did your last job lose you more money than you made in the transaction?

The reason that this happened may be that you didn't put your resources toward quality strategic planning. You didn't focus enough on cash flow and profit.

If the cause of your problems is that you didn't invest sufficiently in the areas of staffing and planning to begin with, scaling back on them during hard times is only going to make the situation worse.

The Importance of Commitment: An Example of Failing to Invest Resources for Planning

On two separate occasions, I coached a client who wanted to turn his struggling business around. He'd had cash flow issues and had large uncollectible receivables that had resulted in a floundering business. He had taken time to plan how to get himself out of the situation, but when it came to executing the plan, he wouldn't commit to the resources required. After about two months, he abandoned the plan altogether, and the company collapsed.

Two years later, he approached me again with a new concept he was working on. He assured me that this time would be different, and we started to

> develop a good strategic plan for his new business venture. However, when it came to doing the work and putting the resources in place, he failed to commit once again. This venture never got off the ground, and I believe he eventually went back to working for someone else to keep a roof over his head.

Being an entrepreneur takes courage and discipline. Make sure that you are willing to invest both the time and resources it takes to get you to your goals. A coach can only take you so far, and then it is up to you to put in the hard work and dedication.

Continue to Learn and Grow

Continuous learning is a passion of mine. I have always believed that if you are not learning, you are not growing. There is always something new and exciting to learn from others.

In my career, I have learned to follow this rule:

Always try to be the dumbest person in the room.

What I mean by this is that you should surround yourself with others who are more informed than you, who have done it before and have broken through to the other side, those who are champions of their own success and have those tidbits of information that can help you get to your goals faster.

Read a book. Devote an hour of learning each day to an area in which you want to improve. Don't try to reinvent the wheel. There are others out there who have already overcome the same challenge that you are currently facing; so, to get to your goals faster, skip the trial-and-error part, and go right to the solution. Devote the time and energy to make investments in your future.

Let's do a little temperature check to see how you are personally doing in this area:

- When was the last time you read a book on how to improve your business?

- Who, in your inner circle, pushes you as an entrepreneur?

- When did you last attend a trade show or a conference that connected you with people or ideas that could lead your business into the future?

- When was the last time you shopped a competitor?

- When was the last time you asked your team members what they would change in the business if it were theirs to run?

- After answering these questions, what are you willing to commit to as you go forward?

The title of this section is *Continuing to Learn and Grow.* When I speak of learning, I'm referring to your personal learning. What I speak of growth, I am talking about continuing to grow your business.

My top three business values are:

- Helping others
- Growth
- Leadership

There is the reason that growth is number two on my list—I am passionate about it!

Think about the state of your business as you read these questions:

- What areas could you improve upon?
- What areas could be more efficient?
- What new product lines could you add?
- Are there any opportunities for expansion?
- Are their new geographical regions that you can tap in to?

If you're reading this book, chances are good that you are involved with a small business. It's likely that there are areas in your business that aren't fully developed or mature yet. If you picked up this book because you are concerned about your cash flow and profit, it is clear that some parts of your business are not working as well as you had hoped.

Here are some important ideas to keep in mind about growing your business:

- Growing means being better off tomorrow than you were yesterday.

- Growing a business has little to do with size; you certainly don't need to have a big business to be successful.

- Growing your business is about keeping the passion alive and keeping the momentum going forward.

GET OTHERS INVOLVED

Once you have your focus in the right area, and your intentions are in place, it's time to get others involved so you can reach your goals faster.

How many people do you involve?

When is the right time to get them involved?

To what extent do you get them involved?

Finding good answers to these questions is key to making your business plan work.

Communicate Your Plan Internally and Externally

It is important to communicate your plan to get everyone on board with your vision for the company and the goals you want to achieve. How you communicate the plan — and to whom — is very important.

Obviously, you need to communicate your plan to your team. This may be done in team meetings, performance reviews, or strategic planning sessions.

Before you proceed, you'll need to answer this question:

When it comes to cash and profitability, what information should you share with the various members of your team?

There are many different approaches to sharing information in a business.

For example:

- For a given employee, some business owners only share KPIs that are relevant for an individual's performance, while others are more open.

- Some entrepreneurs share all information with senior leadership, believing that full disclosure will result in open and honest dialogue that will improve the company's decision-making process.

- Others don't even share their financial account information, even with their accounting team members, because they view it as an invasion of their privacy.

- Some business owners hide cash and profitability information as much as possible, including hiding any difficulties from their external financing and lending partners.

If you want to correct shortcomings you currently have, establishing proper balance and discipline in information sharing is part of the process. There is a right way and a wrong way to approach some elements of sharing information, and we will discuss some examples below. However, no strategy will work in every situation. You will have to assess the specific nature and needs of your company to make these decisions.

As a general standard, I recommend leaning toward creating an environment of trust and collaboration instead of being overly protective. You will tend to get greater and faster results by fostering this kind of environment.

If you don't share relevant financial information with your accounting team, you will handcuff them from doing their jobs properly, which will only make matters worse. However, if you have a large accounting team, you can use discretion in letting your junior personnel know the true nature of your cash situation. Chances are, they are still green and don't understand the complexities of running a business, so they may jump to the wrong conclusions when they see a cash deficit.

In addition, it is possible that disclosing profitability numbers to your whole team—versus just your senior team—can leave you exposed to the risk of your competitors getting wind of your numbers, especially if you are experiencing some employee turnover. Accordingly, confidentiality clauses in your employee contracts are always a good idea.

Without a doubt, hiding key financial information from your lending partners, including banks and investors, is one of the worst things you can do. They will eventually find out anyway, as most require financial reports as a condition of lending you the money in the first place.

Empower Your Team to Drive Performance

What does empowering your team look like?

To answer this question, we'll need to ask another one:

What is your leadership style?

There are lots of different leadership styles, and I think I have had the pleasure of working with most of them over the years. Your individual style and skillset will determine the personality of your leadership. No matter what your style is, it will be your responsibility to empower your team.

Empowering them will require you to manage your staff while keeping high standards, but this does not mean micromanaging. A good leader gives employees the space to use their skills to the best of their ability, allowing them to perform in ways that are most efficient for them, and tapping in to their unique potentials. Micromanaging can severely limit productivity. When you constantly interfere in the performance of tasks, your employees will start second-guessing themselves. In addition, they will stop making decisions without your go-ahead, and before you know it, you will find yourself doing all the work yourself.

However, empowerment does not mean giving your staff free rein. People need guidelines under which they will perform, and guidance to bring things back in line when they are off track.

And remember the adage: *You can't manage what you can't measure.* Your employees need measurements to tell them how they are doing. KPIs, structured meetings, performance reviews, deadlines, and action items all form a basis for management.

The right balance of leadership and management will create the correct environment for empowerment.

Sharing Your Financial Dashboard and Keeping It Front and Center

In your small business, you probably have at least three departments:

- Sales
- Operations
- Finances

The people who head up each of these departments should be carefully chosen. These three areas are the top performance drivers for your business. At the very least, the heads of these departments are the three individuals that you want to share your financial dashboard with, and keep it front and center in your conversations with them. Full disclosure of the challenges and hurdles of your business is required for these individuals to do their jobs properly.

These three department heads are so intertwined with each other that to leave them out of conversations regarding your financial performance is dangerous to the ongoing success of your business.

Without sales knowledge, operations cannot prepare for what is coming down the pipeline. Without operations knowledge, finance cannot predict cash flow requirements. Without profit knowledge, sales cannot determine how much they need to sell, and at what price. There are numerous other examples of how intertwined these three departments are. I am sure you already have experience with most of them.

If you are not currently sharing your financial information with these three individuals, the question becomes not why, but rather:

Are they the right three individuals for you and your company?

It all comes down to trust. The only two reasons you have for not sharing this information with them is either you never knew you had to — and now you know! — or you don't trust them.

Ask yourself these questions:

- Do you trust these individuals to be able to keep sensitive information confidential?

- Do you trust them to be able to work together under a variety of circumstances?

- Do you trust them to work in a collaborative environment in difficult times?

The last thing you want is someone on your team jumping ship because they have been informed there is a leak in the boat. You want them to be able to either patch the leak to keep the ship from sinking, or build a better boat and help steer it toward your ultimate destination.

SEEK EXPERT ADVICE FROM A PROFIT COACH

In this book, we have covered a great deal of material, and most of it has been centered around cash management and profitability.

Does it seem overwhelming?

Business owners, as we have discussed, wear many different hats. With so much on your plate, it can be daunting to take on additional tasks, especially tasks that you do not have the training, experience, or skillset to accomplish on your own. It isn't surprising that many small business owners seek experts for help.

There are three main reasons people give for hiring a coach or other expert:

1. They are stuck and can't seem to get started in the right direction.

2. They want to reach their goals faster; they value time as money.

3. They know what they want, but they do not want to reinvent the wheel; they are seeking an expert who already has a proven method that will achieve the goals they want.

Many experts advertise that they can help you with the strategic direction of your business. They may have different methods of coaching and teaching, and may work within specific parameters and guidelines.

Getting Outside Help to Improve Profitability

When you are looking to hire a consultant to assist you with managing your cash flow and profitability, you will probably be choosing between one of the following three professional experts for your small business:

- A business coach
- A part-time chief financial officer (CFO)
- A profit coach

Let's look at each of these options.

Business Coaches

Business coaches come in all shapes and sizes. There are leadership coaches, executive coaches, and sales coaches, just to name a few. They work with business owners and entrepreneurs on areas such as training, strategic planning, employee engagement, and process and procedural development.

It can be a challenge choosing a business coach because anyone can call themselves a coach. Although classes are available and you can be certified as a coach, the coaching profession is not well regulated yet. Coaching has become a billion-dollar industry, and with the power of the internet, you don't even have to leave the comfort of your home to work as a coach. Of course, the quality of coaches varies. Some of them are quite good, and others are mediocre at best. Some, unfortunately, are so poor that they give the coaching business a bad rap.

It can't be denied, however, that business coaching is an important and growing profession; there is a large and increasing need for coaches in the business world. Small business owners know that finding the right coach can save them both time and money.

Part-Time CFOs

A part-time CFO can be helpful for a small business that cannot afford someone full-time but requires this specific financial skillset. A CFO should have expertise in accounting, operations, and financial planning; have substantial corporate experience; and hold a professional accounting designation. This person will operate your financial department, one of the three departments listed in the previous section of this chapter.

Typically, the CFO will:

- Be empowered to make key management decisions
- Provide high-level financial forecasts
- Manage cash flow
- Manage your shareholder actions
- Negotiate contracts

Given full disclosure of key information by management, a CFO can help mitigate business risk and protect the future viability of the company. A CFO cannot do their job properly without this full disclosure. Being a part-time CFO does not limit the role of the position, as it is still a senior role; it just limits the time involved in that role.

Profit Coaches

How is a profit coach different from a business coach or part-time CFO?

Profit coaches are primarily focused on one issue: the company's profitability. The profit coach is an external advisor who works with your accounting team and leadership team to keep them focused on areas of the business where profitability can be improved. This includes the six foundations of your business mentioned in chapter three—sales maximization, operational excellence, customer satisfaction, employee engagement, finance, and R&D.

The profit coach should act in support of the company's vision and will participate in strategic meetings to help keep the business grounded and growing. A profit coach can also recommend new profit-building frameworks for your business. The profit coach advises various courses of action, but does not make the ultimate decisions and is not hands-on in the business.

How Can a Profit Coach Help?

A profit coach can help your company move its cash position from red to black. They can find ways to help your business become more efficient and disciplined in its spending, improve external financial relationships, and strengthen the overall financial health of your business.

You want to run your business from a position of empowerment and, to accomplish this, accurate and up-to-date financial information is required. One way a profit coach can help you is by building better financial templates so you can receive the reports you require in a timely manner. They can also help your business in real time by focusing on profit performance while it is happening, allowing proactive improvements to be made along the way, thereby maximizing results. A profit coach can also reduce the amount of time you spend on non-value activities.

For a small business owner, a profit coach can help provide clarity, reduce your stress, and move you to financial freedom quicker than you can do it yourself. They are instrumental in creating a culture around profitability. The profit coach can create not just strategic plans, but financial strategic plans with numbers that help and support your business strategies. They help to hold you, the business owner, accountable for following the plan once it has been developed. A good profit coach will understand the financial world as well as the business world and will be able to link the two together.

It is a relatively new area of coaching, and I recommend that when dealing with a profit coach, you work with someone who is certified, with an accounting designation, and has related business experience within your industry. This will give you the best opportunity for success. However, an excellent accountant won't necessarily make a good coach. People skills are also an important factor to consider, as well as a strong desire to help. The right balance must be there.

When Do You Need a Profit Coach?

Profit coaches are not for every business. There should be a specific need and desire for profitability within the organization for it to be the right match. All companies will go through various life cycles and may have seasonal tendencies. There is a time in the life of every business when hiring a profit coach becomes strategically vital. A business owner will engage profit coaches for different reasons, and for different amounts of time, depending on the condition and goals of the company.

For example:

- A profit coach may be asked to help to solve a particular problem the company is having with cash and profits.

- A profit coach may be engaged to improve profitability in general.

- A profit coach may work with a business owner on a specific project.

- A profit coach may be highly involved at the beginning of a business relationship and then taper off to more of a monthly maintenance consultation.

- Profit coaches can be actively involved with a business for years.

The hiring of this coach depends on the needs and goals of the business, as well as how aggressive the company's growth pattern is.

Good profit coaches have cultivated a unique skillset that is aimed exclusively at supporting business profits. They may be able to meet needs that your business has—needs that you may not even be aware of. Different profit coaches may have different methods, and some have their unique offerings, like my own three-dimensional profit model that is described in this book.

Profit coaches tend to live and breathe profit because it is their passion. This passion, in turn, plants a unique seed within any organization that they work with. Because profit coaches have a pinpoint focus—on profit—all their energy is directed in this area. There is power in this kind of focus; it is much stronger than a generic focus, and it is more likely to deliver the results you want.

As we've discussed, small business owners often have trouble getting accurate, pertinent financial information about their own company when they need it, and a profit coach can help in this area. Having your coach directly mentor your accounting team can provide added value for your company. When a profit coach educates your team, they can turn your own employees into mini profit promoters.

In all endeavors, the goal for both the coach and the entrepreneur is to develop a relationship that is supportive and collaborative, and to create an environment of growth, stability, and profitability.

CHAPTER FIVE EXERCISES

- As a leader, how do you link your company's profitability to the inner motivations of your team members?

- For your business, are you ready — right now — to commit time and resources to cash management and profitability?

- Are you pushing yourself to continue to learn something new every day?

- Do you want to grow your business? If so, to what extent?

- What information about cash and profitability are you willing to share with your team? Are there certain individuals who require more information than others? Why?

- Do you have the right people in the top three roles of sales, operations, and finance? Do you trust them?

- Looking at your current business needs, would you benefit from hiring a business coach, a part-time CFO, or a profit coach? If so, which one will you choose and why?

Conclusion

I want to thank you for taking the time to read this book. In doing so, you have invested in yourself and in your business.

Tackling issues of cash flow and profitability can be difficult, and for a business owner, the thought of devoting time and energy to accounting tasks can be excruciating. In writing this book, my goal has been to use my skills as a professional accountant to deliver this content to you in nontechnical terms. I hope that I have brought to light some thoughts and ideas that will help you remove your own roadblocks and barriers, allowing you to become the champion of your own success.

After reading this book, have you determined who is watching your money?

You have read in these chapters that, in most small businesses, there are shortfalls in accounting as it relates to cash and profit, and it is likely that *no one* is devoting sufficient time and resources when it comes to watching your money.

You can change all that. Take control of your business and you will increase your profits and your chances for long-term success as an entrepreneur.

Here is a summary of what we have reviewed in this book:

- We have identified the difference between focusing on what has happened in the past and forecasting for the future.

- We've discussed the difference between cash and profit — cash is currently what you have on hand, and profit refers to your future cash.

- We talked about methods for good cash-flow management and the need to plan for profitability.

- We explained why having cash in the bank doesn't mean you have a successful business. Conversely, we discussed why, even if you do have a successful business, this does not guarantee that you will not run out of cash.

- We have identified various sources and uses of cash, certain areas in your business where you could be hemorrhaging, and how you could put some internal controls in place to stop the bleeding.

- We also explored a unique way to plan strategically that involves my three-dimensional profit model, which is focused on the profit formula, the six key foundations of your business, and the positive proactive results graph that links actions to results.

- The importance of a complete financial plan was also brought to light, as well as how to involve others in that plan.

I hope that the information you read has helped you to see where you need to focus to be successful. I hope you have been inspired to take initiative and move forward with renewed energy in your business.

At the end of each chapter, I have included questions to help you guide your thoughts and get you ready to start taking action. I hope you took the time to complete these questions and have already started making improvements within your business. If not, it's not too late to begin. Don't waste time. Time is money, and this currency keeps us all on the same playing field.

Consider this question carefully:

What are you doing with your time?

What you do will greatly impact what your future looks like.

The next step in your profit journey is to implement what you have learned in this book. If you truly want to turn your company into a results-driven organization, then you need to start working *on* your business, not just *in* it.

If you are having a hard time getting started, commit to taking the following initial steps:

- Invest in having the right senior internal accounting staff on board. They should be capable of creating the reports that will provide you with clarity, vision, and timely information regarding cash and profits.

- Make a cultural shift toward accountability of profit, and include it in your decision-making process.

- Fully engage the heads of your sales, operations, and finance departments in this new aspect of your decision-making process.

- Invest in strategic planning a minimum of once per year, and incorporate the three-dimensional profit model in the process.

- Get rid of the white noise and focus on reports, strategies, and actions that will deliver results.

- Measure the difference between the value added and the cost of each strategic action, and make sure it's a positive one.

- Make sure that your detailed financial plan is a key component of your strategic planning process. Insist that cash flows, forecasted profit and loss statements, and forecasted balance sheets are incorporated into your planning.

- Put budgetary and spending controls in place throughout all areas of your business, including sales, marketing, operations, and finance.

- Invest in outside expert advice from a profit coach when required. The unbiased third-party input can help you see what you don't see, and can initiate proven methods to get you to your results more quickly.

Like any other book you have read in the past, any other seminar you have attended, or any other coaching advice you have received, what you do with that information is entirely in your hands. You will act on it, or you won't. As is always true, your results will reflect the decisions you have made.

On the next page, I've provided you with *Your Roadmap to Profit:* some final questions to start you on your way.

Are you ready to embark on your journey to success?

If so, then your future awaits, and it's going to be a good one!

Your Roadmap to Profit

R: Are you driven by **Results?**

O: Do you have the **Organizational skills** necessary to carry out a detailed action plan?

A: Do you hold yourself and your team **Accountable** at times when it really matters?

D: Are you a **Dashboard thinker,** focusing on those items that really matter and eliminating all the white noise?

M: Can you **Manage** your staff well, giving them guidelines, testing and measuring performance, but empowering them at the same time?

A: Are you **Action oriented** in everything that you do?

P: Are you a **Profit promoter** for your own business?

T: Are you ready to **Transform** the way you think and behave?

O: Are you **Open** to coaching and to learning different approaches that you've never thought of before?

P: Can you link the **Profit formula** to the key foundations of your business?

R: Can you successfully identify the **Roadblocks** in your business?

O: Can you capitalize on the **Opportunities** in front of you?

F: Are you disciplined enough to create a complete **Financial plan** to support your initiatives?

I: Are you ready to **Implement** that plan throughout your organization—in meetings, performance evaluations, culture, and communication?

T: Will you continue to **Test** and measure the progress of that plan, making corrective actions along the way by using key reports?

Are you ready?

Good luck on your journey!

Next Steps

Start your own personalized *Roadmap to Profit* today. For more information about available services, such as profit coaching, part-time CFO work, the Profit Academy, accounting software upgrades, financial health assessments, business-plan writing, and strategic planning sessions, please visit our website at roadmaptoprofit.com or email the author at belynda. debeurs@roadmaptoprofit.com. You can also follow her on Twitter @Belyndadebeurs or on her FaceBook page at RoadmapToProfit.

About the Author

Belynda de Beurs, CPA, CGA

The Profit Coach

Belynda de Beurs is the founder and visionary behind roadmaptoprofit.com, a worldwide transformational profit coaching and profit training academy tailored for growing small businesses.

Belynda has always had a passion for accounting and has never deviated from this career path. She started her accounting education in grade eleven and achieved her professional CPA designation in 1999. Her desire has always been to become a financial accountant working closely with management inside the operations of their businesses.

Most of her experience in the workplace has come from hands-on experience as she has climbed the corporate ladder, eventually reaching a CFO position. During the last fifteen years of her career, she has been working directly with senior management and business owners on strategic and long-term planning.

In 2009, Belynda began offering part-time CFO services, which included future forecasting and strategic planning. She has been very successful, helping one of her clients grow from a $20 million company to a $120 million company in only three years. As part of her unique path to self-discovery, she began to dedicate time to provide coaching services designed to transform potential into profit. Soon afterward, her new vision of the *Three-Dimensional Profit Formula* was born. It is a unique concept that blends simple math with strategic planning. It lays the framework for accountability and engagement, and it delivers massive results.

Belynda continues to provide personalized profit coaching and part-time CFO consulting services, striving to maximize the potential success of small businesses using her profit formula. She has also developed a six-step P-R-O-F-I-T training program for internal accountants to empower them to protect the profit and performance of the companies they work for.

79118173R00102

Made in the USA
Columbia, SC
27 October 2017